PRAISE FOR

Racing Across the Lines:
Changing Race Relations through Friendship

"This combination memoir/discussion guide is solidly based on Plummer's professional and scholarly understanding of diversity issues. She challenges readers to think beyond the workplace to examine personal relations across racial boundaries as one step toward achieving a just society."—*Adrienne Lash Jones, emeritus associate professor of African American Studies, Oberlin College*

"Dr. Plummer's book is an excellent lesson in reality and reason as we struggle to overcome the evil of racism which is almost omnipotent. It is a book that can be used constructively by youth and adults, individuals, groups and institutions, and I highly recommend it."
—*Rev. Otis Moss, pastor, Olivet Institutional Baptist Church*

Racing

across the lines

Changing Race Relations through Friendship

Deborah L. Plummer

The Pilgrim Press
Cleveland

DEDICATION

To My Parents
Phyllis and Leroy
My First Diversity Management Teachers

To My Husband
Mike Bussey
Who Continues to Provide the Lessons

The Pilgrim Press, 700 Prospect Avenue East, Cleveland, OH 44115-1100,
www.thepilgrimpress.com
© 2004 by Deborah L. Plummer

Published 2004. All rights reserved
08   07   06   05   04   5   4   3   1
Library of Congress Cataloging-in-Publication Data

Plummer, Deborah L.
    Racing across the lines : changing race relations through friendship / Deborah L.
    Plummer.
        p.   cm.
    ISBN 0-8298-1602-x (pbk. : alk. paper)
    1. Race relations.   2. Interpersonal relations.   3. Race awareness.   I. Title.

HT1523.P58   2004
305.8—dc22   2004053350

Contents

112417

Acknowledgements

FORTY YEARS AFTER THE Civil Rights Act and fifty years after the *Brown v. Board of Education* decision, race remains a prickly topic for discussion. This book, in part, is the compilation of those persons who were willing to go beyond the prickly and share their stories of friendship and their ideas on contemporary race relations in numerous focus groups. To the many persons whose names are mentioned in this book I am grateful.

A memoir cannot be written without including your family and friends. Gratitude goes to my family and friends who blindly trusted me to write about them as I wrote about my professional and personal experiences.

There are others whose names are not included in this book whose support was critical to this book becoming a reality: Jane Lassar and Kathy Dawson whose advice on publishing outside the world of academia was invaluable; Tonya Strong Charles for her unwavering belief in the viability of this project—your encouragement helped me to believe; Tracy Miller Dotson and Matt Dotson for having so many interracial couples as friends for me to interview; my former faith family of the Sisters of Notre Dame in Chardon, Ohio, for your continued pride in my accomplishments; my current church family of St. Agnes-Our Lady of Fatima parish in Cleveland, Ohio, for being a witness of God's diversity.

Getting an idea from manuscript to reader is a mammoth task. My thanks go to Kim Sadler, my Editor of The Pilgrim Press, and Eleanor Hayes, my publicist, for their guidance and support.

And to all of you who are reading this book—thanks for being a friend!

Introduction

THERE ARE SOME THINGS IN LIFE that might have been considered superfluous in theory, but now in reality have become necessities: Post-It, notes, suitcases with wheels, cable television, George Foreman grills, call-waiting, voice mail, pop-top cans, e-mail, bottled water . . . friends that cross racial lines. Just as traveling becomes easier with suitcases on wheels, understanding and managing race relations in America is easier and less complicated through friendships and socializing. As with Post-It notes, once friends of different races are in your life, what was once considered non-essential now becomes essential—the "nice to have" becomes a "must have." Cross-racial friendships and socializing are that kind of "non-essential" essential.

This book is about America's friendship and socializing patterns discussed through the lens of race and conceptualized from a spiritual framework. It explores patterns of cross-racial socializing and friendships and their challenges and supports. I hope reading this book will support you in examining your friendship patterns and their connection to your spiritual life. Although it is primarily a book about patterns of friendships across racial lines, it is more importantly a book of personal, professional, and spiritual growth—my own and yours.

During my elementary school years from kindergarten through eighth grade, I evolved from being a student in a racially-mixed school to becoming a student in an almost predominantly black school. My best friends at St. Thomas Aquinas Elementary School—Gayle Starling, Cheryl Maxwell, and Debbie Harris—were black. When I graduated from eighth grade in 1965, my parents, being Panamanian and Jamaican, didn't know they were not supposed to flee the inner city with the rest of the white folks and moved us to a predominantly white rural area about thirty miles outside of Cleveland, Ohio.

At thirteen, I found myself a ninth grader in an all-white (really *all-white*), all-girls Catholic high school. Thirty miles away from Gayle, Cheryl, and Debbie, my new friends became Joan, Rita, and Michelle—

all white girls. Although I did not see my black elementary school friends very often during high school, to this day we remain friends. I also remain friends with my white girlfriends from high school. Not surprisingly, this black set/white set racial combination of friends heightened my awareness about racial differences in friendships and patterns of socializing. Along with the usual identity confusion of adolescence, I actively struggled with racial identity resolution. I was often "too black" or "too militant" for some of my white friends—and I "talked like a white girl" and had "been around *them* too long" for some of my black friends.

In 1969, instead of heading to historically black Fisk University with Gayle and Cheryl, as planned, I interpreted Sister Mary Dion's comment that I could do MORE with my life if I answered THE CALL and entered religious life. I became a "black nun" in an all-white community of religious women and lived in an all-white world for the next thirteen years. Here, I learned a lot about white culture and, more important, learned the necessity of sustaining and maintaining my own racial identity. I also came to know how racial identity resolution and interaction with other races needed to be spiritually based.

In 1982, I took a leave of absence from my religious community, loosely maintaining the many white friendships I had made while immersing myself in my black culture. From 1982 until 1986–87, when I was formally released from my religious vows and completing a doctorate in psychology, I used myself as a guinea pig while I researched racial identity development. Today, as a psychologist, university professor, and diversity management consultant, I have incorporated into my professional and personal life the many formal and informal lessons learned over the years about managing differences. I now believe that the only way to really develop personally, to improve community race relations, to build effective work teams, and to live authentically as a Christian, or to live a spiritual life, is by socializing across racial lines. Having friends whose skin color, hair texture, shape of eyes and nose, lip size, cultural values, and world views differ from our own is the key to fuller personal and professional lives. As a person of faith in the Christian tradition, I believe that the diversity of the early Christian community was intended for how church experience is to be lived today. Thus, crossing racial lines in friendship not only promotes personal and professional development but also is the only way gospel values can be expressed.

Yet, I know that we just do not socialize much in mixed-race settings. For most of my white friends, I am their only black friend, and most of my friends who are people of color do not have white friends. As a diversity educator and consultant, I have talked to many people about this topic and have listened to even more. We have had some really interesting conversations, so much so that I felt impelled to write about the topic and widen the scope of the audience.

Thus, this book is an invitation to enter into a dialogue about socializing across racial lines. In this information age, much has been written about dialogue as a form of communication. It has been purported to be the communication structure of the twenty-first century. Used effectively with complex issues such as managing diversity, dialogue seeks to discover, enlighten, join, and engage others rather than to inform, argue, rebut, or debate. Although I have read about and taught the use of dialogue, I have probably only experienced true dialogue a handful of times with my friends. I have to work hard to achieve dialogues in training sessions and classrooms. In order to achieve dialogue with my friends, I have to approach that communication with heightened awareness and clear intention—especially when the dialogue is about the prickly topic of race.

Public discussions of race are usually well orchestrated, as were President Clinton's town hall meetings on race. Race discussions that are not scripted usually quickly move to debate—even with the best facilitation. Thus, most sane people generally shy away from informal public discussions of race relations—unless they are magnificently skilled in group dynamics, or they enjoy the adrenaline rush of a Jerry Springer-type conversation. For the most part, discussions on race in America are inevitable. Human differences, especially those of a racial nature, cross our path routinely in our public life and, for some of us, in our private lives. However, we are quite deft at avoiding discussions and having honest conversations about racial differences. Thus, knowing how to enter into the topic of race through the art of dialogue has become a difficult but necessary competency in our increasingly multicultural world.

Dialogue takes time and requires trust. Time spent with one another and trust are the foundations of friendships. Friendships and socializing shape and support who we are. Despite the fact that I have conducted literally hundreds of training sessions on managing diversity for organizations, I do not believe that race relations in the United States will progress until what we do after five o'clock and on the weekends, especially in our churches, includes a bit of diversity. It is a whole lot easier to create racial understanding in an interpersonal dyad of friendship than in a televised public forum with the Secret Service present.

If the U.S. economy is to remain competitive, dialogues on race are important. As Americans, we have traditionally held a heightened awareness that an educated workforce drives the economy. Thus, attention has been given to the quality of America's educational system. However, less awareness and attention has been given to the fact that a diversity-competent workforce acts as a catalyst for productivity, high morale, and creativity. Now that diversity scholars have connected the dots of diversity to increased dollars, some businesses have taken note. However, while the *theory* of diversity management can be taught in classrooms and training programs, the *practice* of diversity management can only be learned in the school of life—especially life after work hours.

Leading organizations have turned to competency-based learning models in which diversity competencies are considered just as important as competencies in knowledge management, systems planning, negotiation, and conflict resolution. For successful navigation through the twenty-first-century world, knowing how to interact interpersonally and professionally across racial lines is mandatory.

We need these competencies, not only to support more productive workforces but also to survive as fully functioning human beings. That statement may seem extreme to some of you. If you are saying, "Are you telling me that to be personally fully functioning, I have to have friends of different races?" then I have to say, "Yes." I believe that the benefits derived from cross-racial and cross-cultural experiences support us in mastering developmental tasks that, left unattended, would render us incomplete in our personal development. Cross-racial friendships and socializing, I believe, are spiritual acts.

The rationale or motivation for cross-racial friendships is rooted in the spiritual. For some, the spiritual is realized in formal religious practices. For others, the spiritual is lived as a philosophical orientation. Whether the ground for your spirituality is an organized religion or a personal belief system, socializing across racial lines can only be practiced in a spiritual context. Furthermore, if we are to form authentically Christian and other faith-based communities, dialogues on race are important.

Responding to Jesus' prayer that we all may be one requires that these dialogues take place.

I know that many of you agree with me in theory—you have told me so in many focus groups. I also know that most of you believe that socializing across racial lines as a norm will probably never happen—you have told me that, as well, in those same focus groups. In this book, I will report your thoughts on this topic and share with you some of my own experiences of cross-racial socializing.

I will start our dialogue by developing the case for why we need to move beyond monoracial friendship lists. Then we will look at an explanation of the racial identity development and resolution process. We will continue to unravel the racial identity development process in the following chapters as we explore the discomfort we feel in mixed-race settings, the personal struggle to be our true self in mixed-race settings, and the positive results of cross-race risk taking.

When I travel to the cities of New York, Chicago, and San Francisco, I see many racially mixed groups dining in restaurants and in social gatherings. A racially mixed group of friends, particularly in cities like these, may not be unique or rare. Yet, in focus groups on the topic conducted in these cities that span the United States, people repeatedly acknowledged that their friendship groups were not racially mixed. Even members of multiracial churches, who intentionally come together to establish a community, report the difficulty of forming a faith family when different races are involved. These stories are shared in the following pages, along with the barriers that were present in the development of those relationships. Adding to the dialogue is a report of the results of a survey on leisure-time activities given to the focus-group participants. In reading this chapter, you may find that some of your predictions about how we use our leisure time are true and that other predictions are not.

Many believe the racial divide in the United States is only a small gap. Among them are those who have friends across racial lines. Those in this category may find a dialogue about cross-racial socializing unnecessary and inflated. Others, who also believe that the racial divide is closing, may be themselves race-neutral. They may find such a dialogue baffling. There are many, many others whose lives are lived only on one side of the racial divide and are content for it to be that way. The voices of those persons who intentionally and unintentionally never cross racial boundaries in friendships are also included.

The book ends (but I hope the dialogue continues) by presenting the challenges and benefits of socializing across racial lines gleaned from the voices from these differing perspectives. I have framed the book from a spiritual perspective—for it is only from this perspective that any challenges can be diminished and any barriers removed. Each chapter ends with a "Journalogue"—questions for reflection on racial identity in a personal journal and guide questions for a group dialogue session, as well as suggestions for spiritual practice.

As humans, we have a natural tendency toward ethnocentrism—the belief that our culture is the standard by which to judge all other cultures. We also have a natural tendency toward cultural myopic thinking—the belief that our culture is relevant to all others. If we hold a spiritual perspective and the belief that we are all created in the image and likeness of God, ethnocentrism and cultural myopia are not problematic. In the last analysis, we are all an expression of God's diversity. Friends that cross racial lines reflect this truth.

During and after your reading of this book, my hope is that we can keep the dialogue of cross-race socializing alive and perhaps put God's diversity theory into practice.

As Separate as Fingers

The Case for Cross-Race Socializing

MY FRIEND YVONNE IS A WALKER. She walks for miles and miles. When I am feeling particularly athletic, I walk with her. It is at these times that we enjoy true dialogue—those kinds of conversations that take on a life of their own, that start at one point and lead to thoughts you didn't know you could think. It was on one of these walks that we began to discuss the topic of socializing with whites. Although Yvonne and I are both African American women of about the same age, who grew up with similar backgrounds (two-parent, churchgoing, urban families in which education was prized), we have many differences (Yvonne might *really* want to emphasize that we are different). One of our differences is the race of the people with whom we choose to socialize. Although it is not intentional on either my part or hers, my friends cross racial lines while Yvonne's are almost exclusively African American. Our conversation on that particular walk was about why that is so. This book extends that conversation and invites you to enter the dialogue.

I grew up black (actually Negro), of Jamaican-Panamanian ethnicity, Catholic, middle class with above-average intelligence. My family, comprised of Mommy, Daddy, six sisters, and one brother, lived on an all-black street in a black neighborhood in what is now known as the "inner city." I didn't realize until I was an adult that I grew up in the "ghetto." In the 1960s the "ghetto" was about the only place that black folk could live—poor, working class, and professionals all lived on the same streets and within walking distance of one another. We lived next door to the Thomases and I played with the three Thomas girls—Shelley, Toni, and Delores. I knew that compared to the Thomases and the other black families in the neighborhood—the Plummers were different. We were black, but not from the South. We were black, but not Baptist. We were black and in the "inner city"—but Daddy made us stop playing on summer evenings and come inside to watch Time-Life slide shows from his little red slide projector, taking us to Paris and Greece and other exotic places. On Sundays we returned home from mass (not church) and my dad played classical music so that we could "have culture." Don't misunderstand: There were also plenty of doses of cultural blackness in the house— books, music, and lots of entertaining. Along with the ribs and macaroni and cheese, there were rice and beans and plantain. Along with the classical music, there was Motown and jazz. And along with the slide shows of Paris and Greece, we were exposed to African and black history—long before it was popular to be black and proud.

Maybe it is because of the mix of my blood that I find no discomfort in socializing with whites, Asians, Latins, or Native American Indians. Yet, my African American husband, Mike, who resembles the Thomases in his southern heritage, also experiences this same level of comfort. His family experiences, although similar in the structure (inner city, two-parent), were different in their cultural embeddedness. His family never traveled beyond the city limits (even with a slide projector), and his parents did not hold green cards, as mine did. Our personalities are very different and yet, his introversion does not feel discomfited in racially-mixed social settings. If he is not enjoying himself, it is not because of the racial makeup in the room.

I do not know why this comfort exists for some and not for others. And I believe that searching for the answer will only lead to individual responses and not to the general truth of the advantages of cross-race socializing. I certainly do not believe that it is criminal to have a one-race social list. Let's take it further. I do not believe that it is *even necessary* to have friends from diverse racial background. Nineteen-year-old Keila, a student at Howard University, reminded me of a statement by Booker T. Washington: "In all things purely social, we can be as separate as fingers," Washington proposed to his mixed-race audience during the 1895 Atlanta Compromise Address, "yet one as the hand essential to mutual progress." Being "separate as fingers" socially and only coming together when we need to, particularly for economic advantage, seems to have persisted since 1895. Even in his time, Washington was not without his own critics. Many of his "brothers" accused him of colluding with powerful whites in order to gain support. His words and his conservative approach, they believed, served to undermine the quest for racial equality. Yet, many of the black men that I listened to over the past five years sounded very similar to Washington in their strategic approach to dealing with powerful whites. While maintaining a separatist attitude toward whites, Washington secretly funded antisegregationist activities. He is best remembered today for assisting black Americans in rising from economic slavery. Derwin, Steve, and Andrew—three successful black businessmen—tell me that their primary reason to socialize with whites (and really the only reason they could think of) is because it helps them in their organizational life. Like Booker T. Washington, their agenda is clear regarding economic freedom, and they are unwavering in their commitment to helping other black Americans achieve it. In their opinion, for black Americans, socializing with whites is a business necessity.

So, more than a century later, we are still as separate as fingers. In its subtle, covert, and (sometimes) unintentional form, racism continues to exist. Yet, despite that it has been this way for over a century, I believe it is time to revisit our situation of being as separate as fingers.

Perhaps, in socializing across racial lines, we can really share a vision and thus achieve mutual progress. I do believe that socializing across racial lines provides wonderful benefits in your life and enriches you, personally and professionally. In our daily lives, these advantages are rarely brought to our awareness, discussed, or even raised as important. In fact, our educational system encourages us to get to know people of other cultures only as a way to increase our learning. This learning is generally associated with traveling abroad or with having foreign-exchange students in our homes. Rare is the parent who asks his or her child, "Why do you have only white friends?" Or "Why are all your friends black?" Most likely, the question is the opposite for white parents, if the child has more than a token black friend: "Why do you have *so many black friends?* Or for the black parent, "Where are your black friends? Why do you have to hang around with *so many white kids?*"

I began my study of this topic by securing a number of informal focus groups to discuss socializing across racial lines. There were many eager volunteers, and the discussions always continued well beyond the allotted time. I am an early-to-bedder and have a policy about retiring for the night on the same day as I got up. This did not happen when I held any of the focus groups. Many parking-lot discussions occurred after the meetings, and I continued to receive feedback from hosts of the group days later. One host of an all-white group reported that her friends were now teasing (ridiculing?) her about taking applications for friends of different races. For most of these white people, the fact that their friends were all the same race did not even occur to them, let alone the thought that it might be problematic. "Why do I even have to have black friends?" white, forty-one-year-old Louis asks me. At another meeting, black, forty-five-year-old Steven confronts me: "You want to tell me, with what I know about the history of how blacks have been treated by whites in this country, that now I should just forgive them and turn around and be friends with them?" Louis and Steve are clearly representative voices of their respective races. It is no mystery why most people have only a one-race friends list. And Louis and Steve are not likely to rush to fill out any applications to become friends with someone of another race.

Getting and maintaining friendships is enough work without complicating it with the race thing. Besides, people of color would also have to do a lot more of the work in the "Be a Different-Race Friend category"— and again, whites would have it made. Just on sheer numbers alone, until at least mid-century, there will be about seven whites for every person of color. Thus, people of color end up being "THE friend" for many whites. Victor, a young African American male, relates that he is the first black friend of many of his white college friends. He says that when he goes to their weddings, he never has to be introduced. People come up to him and say, "You must be Victor!" How did they know that? he jokingly asks. So, until there is much more parity in the friendship pool, those of you white folks who have more than one friend of color, share the wealth. And once again, people of color, until you are on the friend list of at least seven whites, you haven't done your part to "represent."

Jo, my friend of many years, laughingly tells me that when people come to her house and look at the pictures on her refrigerator, they always point to the picture of my husband and me and ask, "Who are THEY?" Other friends who know who THEY are respond with, "Oh. Those are Jo's black friends." I know that Jo laughs when she tells me that because our friendship has survived so much over the years that to refer to the friendship by race is laughable. Jo and I were housemates for two years after I completed my doctorate, while I saved to buy my own home. Our families became very close during those years, so much so that the Salvatores became like family to me, and the Plummers were family to her. Her Uncle Matt and Aunt Doretta became my "Uncle Matt" and

"Aunt Doretta." Cousins Nick, Dino, Matt, and Tina became my Italian cousins. The Salvatores and Selvaggios were our large Italian family at our family celebrations. I learned to not just throw Prego over boiled spaghetti but to make sauce ALL DAY with Jo and her Mom—and to "turn it" constantly. As a university professor, my summer allowed for more flexibility and more Italian cooking lessons from Mrs. Salvatore. I learned to make baked ziti under Lucretia's careful watch. Mr. Salvatore's job was the "gofer" (pans from the basement, a trip to the grocery for a missing ingredient) and mine was primarily chopping onions, moving the pans, and "turning the sauce," but I learned to make a great ziti.

While watching an episode of the quiz show *Twenty-One* I was amazed at how much knowledge of Italian foods I had acquired just by being friends with the Salvatores. The bonus round for this particular episode had a series of questions about Italian foods. If correctly answered, the contestant would take home an additional $200,000 to their winnings. If I would have been that contestant, that round would have been a cannoli walk for me. The Salvatores had taught me well.

Although separated now by over two thousand miles, Jo and I can still share the "everydays," and we love hearing about one another's daily lives. Despite her geographic distance, our families remain close. I am spoiled when it comes to eating good Italian cooking and compare even the best of Italian restaurants to Mrs. Salvatore's cuisine. After my dad's funeral, the Salvatores lovingly brought over large trays of ribs and fried chicken and pans of baked beans. Sharing food, particularly our cultural foods, reinforces our affinity for one another. We could all benefit from these kinds of feasts.

If the focus groups were an indication of the interest in this topic, clearly there is energy for it, but it appears *not* to be directed toward crossing the racial lines. Outside the group of interracial couples, all the groups convened were either all white or all people of color! People felt that their candor would be greatly reduced in a mixed-race setting. Blacks stated that they would have no problem being candid and genuine in their remarks, but they *knew* that white people would not say what was really on their minds. Whites, for the most part, don't need to think about race very often, so they don't have a lot of practice in expressing themselves on the topic. For them to be thrown into a mixed-race setting to talk about socializing across racial lines would upset an even exchange.

There do not need to be empirical studies to support the claim that socializing across racial lines is uncommon. An informal review of

Americans' racial socializing patterns leads one easily to that conclusion. In our professional lives, we seem to value heterogeneous groups and even find "work friends" of varied racial backgrounds. After work hours, however, the dividing lines are drawn, and it is only with strained effort and with much discomfort that the partying begins. Even diverse faith communities who come together for worship separate socially outside of the church spaghetti dinner. Is it just the differences in leisure-time activities, entertainment choices, and what is considered "fun" that drive races apart or is it something so deeply embedded in our racial beings that it keeps us apart? One could argue that the drive to remain monoracial in our socializing patterns almost follows a developmental pattern, since kids are notably "color blind" in their choice of friends, but adults have racial filters when it comes to establishing friendships.

Popular adult television programs depict this reality as well. It is not unusual to see professionals on programs of mixed racial backgrounds in the same law offices, courtrooms, hospitals, and school settings. However, socializing across races is so rare that when a program chooses to show different races as friendly neighbors or socializing together, this fact is highlighted in television reviews as New Age or even surreal. Judy, an African American corporate woman, believes that television programming is another way that she as a black woman is made to feel outside of society. "Like that stupid *Friends* show; I don't watch it. It makes me feel outside of what is going on. If these people are getting a million-dollars-plus an episode for some crap that I could care less about, it makes me feel not a part of society . . . but that is where I am at," she states firmly. "I think that white people are not forced into my world. If you want to make [mixed-race socializing] a reality, they have to start coming into our world."

I started each focus group by showing a recent advertisement for Jennifer Convertible Sofa Beds. The ad is entitled "Jennifer's Friends" and depicts a group of eleven people (really beautiful, of course), all plopped on "Jennifer," the name given to the sofa. It is obvious that Jennifer's friends are wonderfully diverse—Asian, black, and white men and women are included in this bunch. Fabulous ad—but if Jennifer were not a sofa, would those people *really* be her friends? I showed the ad to several groups of people. They, like me, thought it was a great picture, but unreal. I contrasted the picture of this ad with a picture of the cast from *Living Single*, a Fox Network television show rated number one among blacks until 1998, and a picture of the *Friends* group, a number one-rated show on NBC for ten years. The *Living Single* group is an all-black group, and the *Friends* group is an all-white group. Much more real, people thought, but the Jennifer ad is still very nice.

Is there a problem if people choose to socialize only with others who share their same outer makeup? Isn't it a natural phenomenon that is part of our universe? After all, you don't see goats playing with rabbits—although an occasional cat and dog might enter into a good partnership. Is the fact that the races don't socialize together even an issue worth talking about, let alone writing about?

Well, maybe we should look at the changing demographics. It has been reported that in less than one lifespan, Americans who belong to racial and ethnic minority groups will outnumber non-Hispanic whites. Already, if you walk the streets of New York City or drive around Los Angeles, you experience this projection of racial diversity. Businesses have been preparing for the twenty-first century workforce for more than a decade by providing diversity training and building inclusive work environments in order to remain competitive. There seems to be a compelling business rationale for cross-racial harmonizing in the workplace—but what about after work hours?

Is there not a more compelling reason for diversity than scripture and the social teachings of most religious congregations? Yet, segregated faith communities are the norm. And those congregations that have achieved racial representation find it challenging to have its diversity reflected in its spiritual expression and governance of its practices.

It is said that, on average, most persons only have about one or two really close friends in a lifetime. More gregarious people travel through life with a social group of about six to ten friends. Widening the circle to include friendly acquaintances can take the tally up to about twenty-five. Considering these numbers, there does not seem to be a compelling case for moving out of one's racial boundaries in the search for friends. There seems to be plenty of choices from the look-alike category, and it takes precious time and considerable psychological effort to extend ourselves into the "don't look like me" category.

Also, Americans are busier and busier people. Modern communications provide countless ways to keep us informed and thus ever busier with projects, deadlines, and goals. Time is at a premium—all the more reason that precious leisure time needs to be spent with people we can easily relate to and who share a common understanding of what it means to have fun, relax, and even worship together.

Most people enjoy spending this precious leisure time in activities that do not require much of their intelligence quotient. If learning happens as a result of relaxing and having fun, then it is merely a happy by-product of some good ole' chilling time. Why stretch yourself to have fun? *The Hughleys*, a sitcom starring stand-up comic, D. L. Hughley, depicts the story of an African American family whose financial resources allow them to be able to move into a "better neighborhood"—i.e., a white neighborhood. D. L., as the main character, struggles against losing his black identity and works hard to maintain it for himself and his family. As one of the few television programs that deals with socializing across racial lines, the script is rich with learning. In one episode, a Korean family moves into the neighborhood. D. L. does not get along with the Korean grandfather, who equally dislikes D. L. Racial slurs in the form of stereotypes are passed back and forth. When a covered dish is brought to the Hughley cookout, D. L. just knows there is dog in it. The Korean grandfather, not to be outdone, makes remarks about Hughley's seasoning of collard greens. Finally, the two are forced into a discussion of their differences. Their conclusions about why people do not cross racial lines for friendship: "Maybe it doesn't have anything at all to do with prejudice; maybe we are just lazy."

When we cross racial lines in friendship, it does indeed take work. By definition, the notion of friendship supports relaxation, intimacy, and comfort. Kimili, a twenty-three-year-old African American female, explaining why she found it difficult to have white friends, described a friend as someone with whom you can "just feel like home." Her friend, Myla, underscores the concept by stating that friends are people with whom you can "do a 'number two'" in their bathroom and you don't have to worry about it." For some reason, Myla has never experienced this level of comfort with white folks.

It does not take a group of social scientists (although there are many who make a very good career of it) to tell us that we choose our friends because we have something in common with them. It is natural to assume that those who resemble each other on the physical level would begin the process of friendship selection there. We also choose our friends because of common interests. We might assume then that those who enjoy the same leisure-time activity would find friends from that interest pool. Yet, from a survey of leisure-time choices of racial groups, preferences are definitely individual versus group-defined. For example, despite the prevalent stereotype, all whites are not interested in skiing and golf, and all blacks do not love basketball. Musical tastes also are racially varied. Country-western may still be loved predominantly by whites, but there are a growing number of people of color sashaying to the tunes of the Dixie Chicks.

We will talk more about leisure-time activities in a later chapter. Allow me to concede for now that my simple hypothesis—friends are chosen by interests rather than color of skin—may be plain ole' wrong. I found that whatever the choice of leisure-time activity, the race of the potential friend seemed to trump the fact that we may have similar leisure-time interests. Perhaps Jennifer really has to be a sofa in order to have that many racially diverse friends. Maybe as people, we do remain as separate as fingers.

"As Separate as Fingers" Journalogue

For Personal Reflection:

Reflect on your friendship history: your childhood friends, friends during adolescence, and adult friends. What has been the basis for forming these friendships?

What qualities or conditions help you to feel safe enough to risk a new beginning in a friendship?

Review your friendship list with a racial lens. What meaning do you ascribe to its racial composition?

For Group Dialogue:

How has your understanding of God changed through your friends?

How do you see yourself and your faith community putting God's diversity theory into practice?

For Spiritual Practice:

Heighten your awareness of race by intentionally noting God's diversity in your daily life—at the grocery store, in your work setting, at school, on television, in the newspaper. Be grateful to be blessed with this vision of racial diversity.

—TWO—

Out of My Comfort Zone

Using Your Energy to Socialize

Yvonne walks far. Really far. My first walk with her resulted in swollen hands and feet. I could not even climb the three stairs to her kitchen to get that badly needed drink of water. She had to bring it to me at the bottom of the steps. I do much better now on our walks, and I pride myself on the distance we cover. Now, when we return, I can climb those steps and get my own glass of water.

Because I get absorbed in our conversation, I am often oblivious to how far we have walked. Because I have a lousy sense of direction (even in my own neighborhood), I am often clueless about how I might get back on my own. In the years that I have been walking with Yvonne, I have learned other signs that let me know I have walked outside of my comfort zone: when I realize we are heading toward the mall that usually takes me fifteen minutes to drive to, when there are no longer a lot of people honking and waving at Yvonne (she knows everybody), when I figure out that we have been walking for an hour and it will take another one of those hours to walk back, and especially when Yvonne starts looking at me a bit sheepishly because she knows that I am going to lose it when I discover where we are.

Most of us are aware of the times and occasions when we are out of our comfort zones. Like me and the signs I have accumulated from walking with Yvonne, most people can relate stories of the racial stress that occurs when they have discovered themselves to be "the only one" or "one of a few," especially in a social setting. When they tell their story, they generally do so with some pride at having made it through the experience—just like my pride in being able to climb the steps and get my own water after a walk with Yvonne. Sue, an attorney, speaks about having been one of a few whites at a birthday party for an African American friend. "Remember that?" she says to Donna, her white friend who also was at the party. "We had a good time," she declares, with that pride of "I've done that and lived to tell about it." I know that Sue is very socially adept, and her physical and personal attractiveness supports her sense of comfort in most settings. Yet, she, like most people, experiences discomfort when faced with socializing across racial lines.

Jamain, a twenty-five-year-old African American man states that he doesn't "feel comfortable with whites. They don't understand me. I have to speak two different languages, one at work and one at home. All that extra energy. I've got to repeat everything four or five times. I'd rather stay home. It is like I have to put on a show. I am generally quiet around whites because if I were to show my true colors . . . ."

Those persons who have friends of a different race even feel obligated or duty bound to warn their friend when she or he will be "the only one" at a function. Kimili, an elementary school teacher, talks about inviting a newly made white friend in college to a fashion show. "I wanted to warn her. It's weird, because after that night of the fashion show, our friendship wasn't as close anymore."

Joann, a thirty-nine-year-old white woman, speaks fondly of her best friend, Joy, who is black. Relating a time when they were about to go out dancing, she states that Joy turned to her and said, "I forgot to tell you, you're going to be the only white person there." "Will I be okay?" Joann asked. "Yes," Joy definitively stated. Joann reports that they had a "great time." On the occasion of Joann's wedding, she recalls that the bridal party members were all going to a spa for facials, hair styling, and so forth. Her friend Joy, a member of the bridal party, asked Joann, "Am I going to be okay?" Joann *guessed* that her friend was not likely to suffer any overt racial discrimination, but was unsure about unsuspected racial discomfort. Joann is intuitive enough to point out the difference in the "Let's go dancing" episode and the bridal-party spa day. Joann tells me, "I didn't think to bring it up. She [Joy] is more aware of it [racial discomfort]. She brings it up."

Being out of their comfort zone has become so much a part of the daily experience of many people of color that the experience has become normalized. This does not mean that discomfort does not exist—just that it is normal to feel uncomfortable. Similarly, whites who have lived outside of their racial world experience discomfort. When my friend, Father

Mike, who has been a white pastor of a predominately black parish for fifteen years, finds himself in an all-white setting, it is now an unusual experience for him. After a white friend from outside of the parish invited him to a social gathering, his first remark to me upon his return was that there were only white people at the party. "It was odd to be only with white people." I smiled when he said this, thinking the other (white) guests had not given that fact a first, second, or even third thought.

Because my life has continually afforded me "the only one" status, I have gotten pretty used to this discomfort—never comfortable, but *used to* it. Why, with all that practice, am I still not comfortable? Psychologically, we know that identification is a key foundation of communication. I recall the numerous times when I have been at a predominantly white professional gathering, or just shopping at a predominantly white mall with a white friend, and we have passed someone who is black. The "sister" or "brother" and I are quick to say hello. "Do you know them?" my white friend will ask. "No," I reply. The really astute white friends will say with some frustration (especially if they are progressive liberals), "Then they just said hello to you because you are black." "Yes," I reply.

If the physical similarities aren't immediately visible, it takes some work to sort out how we should get the conversation going. The question of how then to build a friendship becomes even more of a challenge. All my years of living with white folks have given me a repertoire of subjects to talk about with them. However, most of my racially different friends do not have a ready bag of introductory topics and it is just too much work to start up a conversation with someone who doesn't share the same racial background.

An exercise we have used in the Diversity Management Program called the quadrant experience illustrates the great amount of skill and competencies, as well as self-knowledge, necessary for creating a dialogue across racial lines. The race-gender quadrant model, used by Cathy Royal and other staff members in the National Training Laboratory's (NTL) diversity facilitation skills workshop, involves dividing a learning community into race and gender quadrants of white men, white women, men of color, and women of color. The staff member tapes masking tape onto the floor of the room, dividing it into four sections. During the exercise, the participants sit in their race-gender groups, discussing a variety of topics—and then the dialogue is opened across the quadrants. It is amazing to see the kind of energy this experience generates and is sad to see how little time it takes for racism and sexism to be imported into the dialogue. We only conduct this exercise with seasoned professionals, and we make sure that there are more than the usual number of faculty members present to facilitate and monitor the experience. The effect on the students is profound and long lasting. Having come into a graduate program possessing a certain level of diversity competence, these students are easily convinced by this experience that even a seemingly simple dialogue across racial lines takes an incredible amount of psychic energy and stamina.

For most of us, cross-race dialogue takes so much work because as children, we were rarely taught the skills to help us negotiate a racially diverse world, nor did our parents model socializing across racial lines. We often hear it said that kids don't see color. Yet, as a social scientist, I know that this is not true. Kids do see color, name it, and even talk about it. What they do not do is attach to this label all the social messages that we have learned to place on race as adults.

My friend and colleague, Christina Callos, is from Greece. We have conducted many diversity-consulting projects together. As the mother of five children, she has many diversity-affirming stories about raising kids. She tells me that her son, Yiannis, has a friend who lived on the next block. Harry was African American and he and Yiannis were in the same kindergarten class. She recalls a neighbor asking her, "What is Yiannis doing with a black kid?" It seemed like a strange question to Christina. Her son also had another friend, Daniel, who was black. One day Yiannis reported to her "Daniel's mom's stomach is brown. She had shorts on, and I saw her stomach, and it is brown." Yiannis had never noticed that his best friend Daniel was also brown.

At my niece's fourth birthday party, I watched her excitedly answer the door as her guests arrived for her first overnight pajama party. Living in a racially-mixed neighborhood and attending a racially-mixed preschool, her little friends looked like a United Nations parade as they came through the door. The mothers stood around with my sister and watched the girls squeal and laugh as my niece introduced her friend to me. "Aunt Debbie, this is my friend, Michelle, she's Chinese . . . . See, look at her slanted eyes," she said pulling at Michelle's eyes to demonstrate just how slanted they were. We all held our "well-trained racial breath" to see what might happen next and watched the two children merrily walk to the bedroom, holding on to each other for dear life. Kids do notice difference.

They just don't attach derogatory meaning. Slanted eyes are slanted eyes. Beautiful and interesting.

If we get this race thing right as kids and don't attach labels and stereotypes to racial differences, why do we so strongly and unyieldingly hold on to these labels and stereotypes as adults? I heard in the focus groups I conducted—and I hear a lot in my professional training groups—about the different values that various racial groups are assumed to hold. People make assumptions about a race's value system and worldview based on their friendship list. The races, as a category, do not know each other very well, and they make all kinds of assumptions about each other's reality.

For the most part, people of color know a lot more about white culture (the default value) than whites know about non-white cultures. "I find it odd that they know nothing about me and I know everything about them—and we grew up together," Janice, a twenty-five-year-old African American states. Janice, like so many of her counterparts, may have lived in a black section of a predominantly white suburb, but she went to racially-mixed schools, where she and other blacks encountered whites on a daily basis. I heard several times in the young adult focus groups of African Americans that in referring to what they believe and know about people of color, whites, as twenty-five-year-old Dwight says, "Just don't know any better."

Whites generally are working to erase old tapes planted by parents and the media about what people of color do and believe. Toyia, a twenty-eight-year-old black MBA student, states, "There are a lot of things about me that I know they don't understand and I *know* there are a lot more things about them that I do understand. I really value the moments when I get to say, 'No, it is not that way'—telling them the difference between you and me. They just don't realize it."

Although many older people of color are tired of "educating whites" about the race experience, younger adults and teens of color consider it just part of living in a real world. "Okay, school's in session" is what thirty-one-year-old Lawrence thinks when racial issues come up at work. Meiva, a fifteen-year-old black teen, tells me that she watched a recent episode of *Real World* with a group of mixed-race friends. After the program, she welcomed her friends' questions about her hair and her views on social issues. Meiva and Mercedes, another black fifteen-year-old, tell me that at their age, they still feel a level of comfort with their friends about the subject of race. However, they are positive that the comfort level will change in college and especially in the work world. "We have a friend, Harry, who is Korean. We say to him, 'Shut up, you stupid Korean.' He laughs. It will get harder as we get older. In college, it will change. There is more reality there, without school to protect you."

As we get older, trust becomes an issue in choosing our friends of a different race. Thirty-two-year-old Gilbert, an African American, believes that "blacks and whites distrust each other because of the history." His navy experiences overseas taught him that without the historical baggage, the relationships between whites and people of color in the United States would be very different. So, he doesn't bring a lot of that kind of baggage to his relationships with whites. Similarly, Linda, a forty-one-year-old African American teacher, believes that you "can trust white people. They have to do something to make you feel comfortable sometimes, but you can trust them."

However, most people embedded in U.S. culture cannot help but internalize all the racial residues of history. Socializing and having friends that cross racial lines, Louis believes, is a "function of where you live and what you do for a living." Sue believes it is also a function of age. "My grandparents, [had no friends of color] . . . my parents less so [had some racially diverse acquaintances]." Fifty-five-year-old Janet, a white marketing executive, reports that growing up, she was very aware of racial prejudice in her home. "I am a product of my upbringing, yet I do have black friends. I am not being prejudiced against race. I am very selective about my friends—it doesn't matter what color they are. They have to have the same moral upbringing, values, financial status, and educational level as I have." Barbara, a forty-year-old real estate agent, feels similarly. "When I look at some of the [television] shows—I liked Cosby—I could relate to what they taught their kids. Some all-African American shows today I can't relate to. Some all-white shows as well. It is a question of values and upbringing." Regardless of race, all persons agreed that how they were raised influenced whether or not they crossed racial lines in making friends.

As a young girl, thirty-nine-year-old Italian American Joann recalls learning about differences. "My aunt's girlfriend, whom she met at a beauty salon fifty thousand years ago (and they are still best friends), would come for holidays. And I, being very young, didn't understand what Hanukkah was or why she didn't celebrate Christmas. Tata—which was "aunt" in Hebrew—is what we called her. So she was like an aunt, but not blood. So those kind of things were incorporated into our home—the differences." Now, as an adult, it is easy for Joann to have friends that cross racial lines and not feel discomfited by difference.

Even when we grow up in welcoming, inclusive homes, it is easy to have our comfort levels threatened. This discomfort usually increases in adolescence. Aaron, a thirty-something African American man, recalls growing up in Columbus, Ohio, and having an equal share of black and white friends. "It was never an issue for me. Yet, other black friends assume that if you have white friends, you don't want black friends."

Pamala, a Chicago mother of two biracial children, states that it is easier to be "more relaxed in the parental structure when you are younger—sleeping over, trading clothes, etc. It is much harder as you grow up, when you really have to be cool to socialize." I interpret this to mean that (just as the research tells us) when you are young, you are not quite so discerning about who your friends are—being in close proximity or owning some material possession does the trick. I can be friends with you because you live next door or down the street, or because you have Nintendo with the latest Sega Dreamcast CD. But as we get older, if our differences and all the meanings attached to those differences are in the forefront, then I would rather travel across the city to socialize with someone like me and get my own Xbox.

Pam, a white mother of three who lives in a small, predominantly white township just outside Cleveland, has made some progress in dealing with racial discomfort developed when she was a child, but she struggles with how to "teach" her children about racial diversity. "How do I introduce my children to that when they are not around it? I can only tell them how I feel. When I grew up, they [her parents] didn't even talk about it."

Not talking about "it" led to a high degree of discomfort with racial differences, I am sure, for Pam and countless other white Americans. It rarely occurs to Pam that she is living in a neighborhood that lacks diversity and because of that, will have to "work hard" to help her kids experience racial differences outside of what the media present. She, like most others, makes the assumption that to live in a decent, crime-free neighborhood, where the property values increase and the school system is excellent, means that it has to be an all-white neighborhood. Yet, Pam strongly agrees that having the competency to navigate an increasingly multiracial world successfully is something that she wants for her children. Unfortunately or fortunately, parents have to be role models in the area of racially-mixed friendships. If kids never see their parents with different-race friends, no matter what is *said* about appreciating and valuing racial diversity, the message will be hard to put into practice. As my niece Mercedes told me, "It is sad when you hear people say that the closest they come to colored people is color TV."

Being Catholic promoted a natural cross-racial social list for my parents, though this was not always the case for all-black Catholics. (I have come to realize in my adult years that my St. Thomas Aquinas experience in the 1960s was a special one.) It was natural for me, growing up, to see white ladies in our house from the Ladies Guild and white men visiting (less often) from the Holy Name Society. We always knew, though, that it was a church function that brought these folks into our home and felt the difference from the real parties that my parents had at New Year's and on birthdays. I wasn't comatose when a white person was in our living room, but I never experienced the same ease and comfort as when there were blacks or other people of color in that living room. The message that it left for me, though, was that somehow God intended for us—whites and people of color—to come together, despite the fact that Sunday mornings still remain the most segregated hours in American society. I believe that crossing racial lines is a spiritual act. It takes the virtues of faith and courage to move out of those preset comfort zones. It is that hard. No one else but God could help us do it.

"Out of My Comfort Zone" Journalogue

For Personal Reflection:

Reflect on your level of comfort with others in racially-mixed social groups. What allows you to feel at ease? What brings anxiety?

What settings provide you with the company of other races? Work? Church or faith community? Community groups? Entertaining in your home?

What personal skills do you believe you have that allow you to benefit from mixed-race environments?

For Group Dialogue:

1. By your actions and practices (rather than written statements), what is your faith community telling others about the value of diversity?

2. What conversations are you *not* having about race in your community?

For Spiritual Practice:

Be aware of the virtues of faith and courage in a racially-mixed social setting.

—THREE—

Growing Up with a Race
Racial Identity Development

I THINK YVONNE THINKS I think too much. In fact, I *know* that Yvonne believes this, because she has told me so straight out on several occasions. At other times, she just gives me a really weird look. On some occasions, while we have been out walking she has told me that black people don't think the way I do. When I remind her that I am black, she amends her statement to an assertion that I am the *only* black person who thinks that way. Since I am one hundred percent confident that my dark, dark-brown skin, multi-textured hair (kinky, curly, straight, wavy, and nappy), and full nose and lips make me at least physically black, I wonder what it is that provokes Yvonne to make these comments. Don't get me wrong. I'm not mad at her for making them—the comments just make me think more.

During my adolescent and young adult years, I struggled a great deal with what it meant for me to be black. As a teen, I was the only black kid in my high school class of two hundred girls. After graduating from high school, I entered a religious community of Catholic nuns. Since I wore full religious garb at the time, I was quite an anomaly. "Gee, I've never seen a black nun before," was how I was most often greeted. People never even had time to get themselves together and even try to act as if they had some manners when they saw me. All their unedited remarks just came stammering out of their mouths. For the thirteen years that I was part of that religious community, I not only embraced a non-traditional lifestyle but also muddied my identity as an African American so completely that by the time I left, getting to know myself racially had become a major goal.

Being one of the few black nuns in the United States and my gregarious personality put me in high profile positions when it came to publicity and validation for the church as an open door, but like the Jennifer sofa advertisement, it was very nice—and also unreal.

It comes as no surprise, then, that my area of research when I became a university professor was racial identity development. How people come to know and embrace their race—be it black, white, Asian, or Native American Indian—captured my attention then and still does today.

Racial identity development is a process that occurs for all people, regardless of their ethnicity or culture. Unlike other areas of identity development—social, personality, cognitive, or physical—the subject of racial identity received little attention until the late 1960s. I recall dancing and feeling empowered by James Brown's song, "Say It Loud, I'm Black and I'm Proud." I also recall feeling a bit embarrassed and ashamed that I was saying the word *black*. I had been Negro all my life and had used the term with great pride, because we had now been assigned a more scholarly term than "colored." The only time I heard *black* was when it was an adjective attached to a derogatory phrase used when someone was mad at someone else. "You black _____" (as in Oedipus Rex) or "You black _____" (rhymes with witch). Now the word was in a number one hit being played on the radio and people were singing it—even in the presence of white people!

Having a race is more than the demographic category that we get to check off on all those forms. Actually, there is really no such thing as "race" outside of the human race, but we act as if there is, despite what scientists and anthropologists have purported for years. Recent research suggests that all human beings share over 99 percent identical DNA. Racial identity, then, is the psychological connection with one's race, rather than the mere identification with skin color or demographic category. People seem to inherently understand this concept and do not need researchers and scholars to tell them about it. Most people of color groups have terms that refer to persons whose demographic racial identity does not match their avowed psychological or racial identity. These are the folks who don't keep it real and are fakes. In the African American community, you are called an "Oreo." You are a "Lemon" or "Banana" if you are Asian, an "Apple" if you are Native American Indian. Mexican Americans refer to the racially confused among them as a "Tio Thomas" (Mexican Uncle Tom) and Jewish people refer to a marginal member as a WASH (white Anglo-Saxon Hebrew). White adolescents who prefer to act more like African American teens are called "Wiggers." There are probably many more racial terms of which I am not aware, as I have been told on several occasions that I, myself, am really not "black." Frequently, two of my godsons count me when they refer to the number of white people present in the room. Paul and Jerome are about as serious as their teenaged minds allow them to be when they say I am not black. My "not being black" is based on the fact that I speak standard English, live in the suburbs, and make Kool-Aid with spring water. They often refer to our pastor and friend, Father Mike (who is white), as just "light-skinned," because they truly see him as their spiritual and psychological father. So, race, as the scientists and anthropologists have told us, is not genetically based but more experientially driven. At least, the way that it plays out in our everyday life has very little to do with a demographic category.

All of this speaks to the essence of racial identity. It is a process of group identity that is distinct from our other identity roles. How do we learn it? We pick it up naturally—it is in the air that we breathe as Americans. As kids, we learned it from what our parents said when they watched the news and witnessed someone of the same race do something negative or positive. I can still hear my mom talking to my Aunt Rene and saying, "Girl, he didn't just say that in front of white people!" As an adult, I remember seeing her jump for joy when Tiger Woods won the Masters because "Whatever he is, he's not white!"

We also learned much about racial identity in school. School, for me, had always been a place of great enrichment, not just from what was in the textbooks or on the blackboards but more from the interactions of the whites, blacks, and Puerto Ricans who comprised my elementary school classrooms. Here is a sample of that learning: I was in about the third grade in health class. Sister Mary Ruth was teaching us about personal hygiene. The question was, How often should you wash your hair? Since the question followed, How often should you brush your teeth? and that answer seemed to be the same for all the races in the room, I didn't think twice about a possible variation in responses to this question about hair washing. Still, because I knew that white people washed their straight hair more often than the members of my household did, I thought I would give a conservative response of every week, stretching it from the usual black hair norm of the time of about every two weeks (this was the time of the hot-comb hair press, before the days of easy chemical hair relaxers). Thank God, Sister called on white Judy Schwelgien who proudly proclaimed, "Every other day" and received a great big smile and excited singsongy, "That's exactly right!" from Sister. God had saved me from being embarrassed. We black girls congregated after class to talk about what life must be like for someone to be able to have the time, energy, and resources to wash their hair every other day. What I learned about racial identity that day was that white people were clearly the norm. Poor Sister Ruth probably would have thought me barbaric had I or any other black kid in that room that day been called on to answer the question. Yet, the lesson I was taught by that interchange was one that served me much better than any information on hair washing. I learned that racial identity shapes our world and influences our thinking and behavior. Today, as I watch many white women get their hair done at Studio Taylor, the salon where I get my weekly manicure, I am wonderfully amazed that many white women struggle to tame their hair just like many women of color. I watch in awe as Nancee Taylor, the salon owner, transforms strands of hair into what I always thought were a "wash and go" look for white women. I ask my friend and manicurist, Denise, about the process. "They do all that with just a blow dryer and a brush?" Denise educates me and I educate her, Nancee, and the other stylist who were intrigued by my natural hairstyles. We talk about products—what some whites can use and not use, do and not do with their hair. We have the same conversation about black hair care. What I have discovered is that the norm for hair washing and styling is as varied as individuals.

I wonder what kids are taught in classrooms about hair washing and grooming today.

NeCole Cumberlander is the creator and owner, along with her husband Orlando, of Noire et Blanc, a salon and day spa. The salon's name, which is French for "black and white," was intentionally chosen to reflect the multicultural styling for which the salon is noted. Nicole's vision for such a salon began early in life. "When I did hair, as far back as high school, I did my friends' hair—black friends and white friends." As she grew older and left college to make a career as a stylist, she kept the vision alive. She thought, "I would really love to see and work in a salon that was truly multicultural. This was the goal and that is how Noire et Blanc was born. I wanted some place that was ultra chic." Her salon today is indeed ultra chic. Described as a sleek, multicultural, unisex salon and spa with a focus on customer service, it attracts customers from all over the world because of the renowned Cleveland Clinic, located across the street from the salon. "People say, this is so nice, and they are really surprised that it is an African American-owned salon. But that is actually kind of sad that people say that, because it is not the norm, and it should be."

Building and maintaining a multicultural salon is quite a challenge for NeCole. She has difficulty convincing black clients that her white stylists are competent to do their hair. NeCole's warm personality, interpersonal skills, and good business etiquette allow her to sail through most of these ordeals. Her greatest challenge, however, comes from retaining white stylists. In the interview process, NeCole is candid about the reality of working in a salon where whites are the minority. She finds that most white stylists who work there must confront issues of race they had previously never encountered. They find out that they might not have been as open-minded as they thought and perhaps are somewhat prejudiced. Sometimes, these disturbing thoughts prevent them from continuing to work at the salon.

Undaunted, NeCole strives to achieve a goal of a racially mixed staff.

> Some days I get really frustrated. I am sick of it. [I tell myself] I'm just going to stop looking. If I have a salon full of all black stylists, then so be it. If that works, that works. But that wasn't the vision. The vision was to have a truly multicultural salon. I'd love to have some Hispanics and some Asians. I'd like a little bit of everybody in here. That was the goal. That was the vision. And for whatever reason—and I still don't think I have quite put my finger on it . . . I mean, I've tried to make sure the customer service was the utmost. I tried to make sure the ambiance was good and the surroundings clean, that the salon was up-to-date. I know the salon looks as good as or even better than a lot of salons—black or white—but that is not enough.

Despite the challenges, NeCole holds to her vision. She hopes to open two more salons and possibly a beauty school. All her projected salons will have a multicultural emphasis. Her philosophies of "hair is hair" and "a good stylist cuts off half her business by only knowing how to do the hair of one race" are fundamental. She had really good mentors during her training. At twenty-one she was on a national design team for Paul Mitchell and traveled extensively. She found her niche in multicultural styling and teaches these skills nationally. The seed of her vision, however, she states, goes back to her family and the upbringing they provided for her. "They were pro-black but not anti-white. I was always taught that people are people. From day one, growing up, I remember choosing friends of different races."

We are indeed taught about racial identity when we are told with whom we may or may not socialize in our leisure time. I vividly recall the confused look on the face of a new black sophomore girl when she arrived at the racially-mixed high school where I taught. She explained to me that her parents sent her to this school specifically so that she would *not* hang around with other black students. She was told to make friends only with the white kids, to avoid trouble, and to be able to achieve. Try responding to that in the three minutes we had to change classes.

At that time, this teenager's message was not as horrifying as it would now appear. It was a sad message but not horrifying, when you consider the racial identity resolution process for many people of color. For some people of color, the journey of discovering their racial identity first begins by identifying with those who are white. Historically and to a great extent even today, white Europeans in the United States have dominated or greatly influenced what is considered the norm in U.S. society. (Recall the norm for hair washing.) People inherently have a sense of wanting to belong and to fit in. Thus, it would make sense for a minority person who was growing up to identify with or to take cues about his or her behavior and thought from those in the majority who set the norm.

Educational systems and organizational life are designed around the customs and beliefs of majority culture. What is good, correct, proper, right, moral, sacred, and holy all come from the dominant culture. For those persons of color not firmly embedded in the culture of their racial identity group, the racial socialization process will most likely be that of white culture. Others, aware of their skin color difference, yet who find their behavior and thought aligned with those of the dominant race, experience what noted scholar William Cross calls "race neutrality." For these persons, their racial identity is not central or core to who they are. It is placed in the background. I am a person who happens to be Hispanic, or black, or Asian, or Native American Indian. In other words, being a person or a human being is primary. Race is secondary or a neutral factor in my life.

However, people of color with race neutrality spend a great deal of energy trying to keep race neutral. A former colleague of mine, who is obviously a person of color who has a coffee complexion and nappy hair (not curly, wavy, or kinky but *nappy*), insisted on *not* being referred to as black. He wanted the freedom to claim his entire racial heritage—Native American Indian and Hispanic. Somehow, *all* never included black (which the rest of his family boldly claimed). He wasn't confused about race or racial identity—he just wanted people to think of him first as a human being. Yet, race was always alive for him. He didn't want to live in a black neighborhood, preferred to date only white women (they understood him better than women of color), and only wanted to work in environments where there were few people of color (places where people were "more professional"). Thus, he worked harder to *not* make race an issue in his life than he would have if he simply owned his blackness!

For most people of color, at some point in the racial identity resolution process, the impact of racism is felt. Santiago, an experienced attorney, lives with his wife and four children in a rather affluent neighborhood and by most U.S. standards lives an exemplary life as a practicing Catholic. By all standards, he is doing the right thing and raising his kids in the right way. Yet, he shares with me his anxiety about having "the talk" with his teenage daughter who is starting to date. "The talk" goes something like this. "Honey, we know that you are a good person and you can do anything and achieve anything you want in this life. We are proud of being Puerto Rican, but we need you to know that some people will find it a problem when Johnny says that he wants to take you to homecoming. Now, we like Johnny and don't have a problem with you and Johnny together, but just so that you are aware . . . Do Johnny's parents know you are Puerto Rican?" Not to have armored his daughter with "the talk" would have made him negligent in his own eyes as a Latin parent.

For many people of color, the response to racism has greatly influenced their racial identity process in such a way that they reject or simply have a strong preference for remaining embedded with or encapsulated in their own racial group. Thus, the racial identity resolution process is satisfied by eliminating or minimizing contact with members of the dominant race. For these persons, all professional and personal activities occur with members of their own race. They become imbued with all that represents the essence of their race. I recall when my very gifted niece, Marie, reached this stage of development. Suddenly she "became black." Her Christmas wish list that year featured such items as *The Miseducation of the Negro* and African mud-cloth pillows. Everyone also got African-centered gifts from her that year. She began witnessing to the family about the joys of being black—no more white stuff for her! Today, Marie's friends resemble the Jennifer sofa advertisement used with my focus group research that depicts the multiracial nature of the United States. Somewhere along the line, people of color get the race thing together, and racial identity becomes stabilized and integrated into their lifestyle. Their racial identity is fully owned and accepted, and thus may appear not as salient in their life. Yet, it is so seamlessly integrated into their being that expressions of their racial identity are natural and easily apparent to others through their manner of speaking, customs, practices, manner of dress, and so on.

Racial identity becomes integrated not only into one's lifestyle but also into other aspects of one's personality and other dimensions of diversity. Surprisingly (to me), I looked and acted most ethnic (natural Afro, African-inspired clothing, African décor in my home) when race was not as salient in my life but more deeply internalized and part of my being than it ever had been before. When I was the "black nun" and probably the most racially confused that I have ever been in my life, race was always central to my everyday experience—largely because I lived in a world devoid of colored faces. I used to say that if Toni Massey (the only black girl in the school) were absent from school that day, then I would not have seen another black face all day. Constantly hitting the race boundary, I was always faced with the visibility of my race and I thought about it a lot more than I ever do today.

For white people, the racial identity process journey is a bit of a challenge. It is easy to conceptualize oneself as the norm as a member of the dominant race. It is very much like a computer system in which the default value is already set. White European Americans are pretty much the default value in this country. American cultural norms have been rooted in an amalgamation of European backgrounds and ancestry. History, education, corporate policies and procedures, and leadership in this country have all been determined and influenced by white culture. Thus, it is easy for white Americans never to have "whiteness" in their awareness or perhaps never to have struggled with being different or with seeing themselves represented in the world. I hear and witness this often in my professional and personal life. White often means a *not*. I'm not black. I'm not Asian. I'm not Hispanic. I'm not Native American Indian. I AM AMERICAN.

Whites run like the wind or quickly change the subject when the consciousness of being white is raised. It is changed so quickly that you could forget that the entire civil rights movement ever happened. I believe this is because whites intuitively sense that it means they will have to say or do something about the privileges and entitlements afforded to them as people with white skin in the United States. So, all you white folks, stop and listen. No need to run or change the subject, what people of color want most is the acknowledgment that discrimination occurred and that as a result, people of color suffered and whites were afforded privileges. You need not defend it, excuse it, or apologize for it (apologies are nice, however). Simply acknowledge it as a fact—just as we can all see that the sky is blue.

At a recent Martin Luther King Celebration sponsored by the Catholic Diocese of Cleveland, Ernest Green, one of the students known as the "Little Rock Nine"—who integrated Central High School in Little Rock, Arkansas, in 1957 following the *Brown v. Board of Education* case—was the keynote speaker. His speech chronicled a period in our country's history when overt racism was poignantly present. With specific examples, Green delineated its residual effects on contemporary society. It was not a depressing speech but one full of hope, as he encouraged us all to continue to join with each other in making Martin Luther King's dream a reality. Although his speech was engaging, what was particularly notable was the response given by Cleveland Bishop Anthony Pilla. Bishop Pilla was asked by the master of ceremonies to make some closing remarks. He stated that he was struck by the hope and successes evident in the lives of Ernest Green and the other African Americans who had been civil rights activists at the time, but he asked those gathered to remember that the successes did not come without pain. Further, he wanted to acknowledge to us—African Americans—that not only society but also the church—our church—had been responsible for our pain. WOW! Those words were worth the price of admission and then some! Bishop Pilla's apology was later made even more public during the 2002 Southern Christian Leadership Conference. The landmark civil rights group held its annual conference in Cleveland where Bishop Anthony Pilla received a standing ovation when he expressed repentance for past racism. "I just want to welcome you to Cleveland, and I want to say this very carefully, as brothers and sisters . . . for whatever we [the church] have done in the past to not live up to that relationship, I apologize." Acknowledgment is a powerful healer. The simple act of acknowledgment helps create a world in which racism is eradicated and privilege is afforded to everyone, regardless of skin color.

My friend and neighbor, Phil, says it well. He believes he enjoys a lot of privilege—"I'm white, I'm male, I'm a physician, I'm tall, and I'm bald." (He assigns great status to "tall and bald.") He also states that he is not willing to give up any of his privileges. In the same breath, he further states that he would work like hell to make sure that in his personal and professional lives, privilege is something everyone has, regardless of skin color. He lives that out by his intentional choices of living in a racially-mixed neighborhood and working in a predominantly black clinic.

The awareness of privilege and entitlement, and the acknowledgment that these conditions have been afforded those in this country who have white skin, lead to a rejection of covert racist beliefs and of the implications and ramifications attached to privileged whiteness in this country. There is recognition of difference in treatment of whites and people of color in this country and a focus on how whiteness brings privilege. For example, Walt, a white male friend, shared with me a conversation he had with a police officer when he was pulled over for not fully stopping at a stop sign. He argued successfully with the officer about the ridiculous nature of his attempt to ticket him and humorously accused him of being overzealous. At the end of his story, he stated that he was acutely aware that he could have never gotten away without a ticket—and more important, with what he said—had he been black. What was in my friend's awareness was privileged whiteness.

When whites fully embrace a white identity divorced from the sense of privilege and entitlement rooted in skin color, they are quick to challenge any system that supports inequality, oppression, and social injustice. They "get it." They understand the historical residues that affect people of color and they keep this awareness in their consciousness.

Trevor is a thirty-six-year-old African American man whose baby face and youthful demeanor belie his age. He is a person who by most standards would be considered conservative in his dress, behavior, and thinking. His uniform for work is a dark suit, white shirt, and tie, and for casual days, khaki pants and polo shirts (all solid colors). Sensible brown or black shoes, a close-cropped haircut, and round-framed glasses complete his ensemble. You get the picture; Trevor would more likely fit into the nerd category than the thug category. His only "out-of-the-box" behavior is that he owns and rides a motorcycle on social occasions. There, however, was one other such occasion. Trevor was approached in a parking lot by a police officer about his bike after he and his (white) friends had dinner at a predominantly white (and worked hard to remain that way) restaurant. I'll make a long story short since you probably already know how it ends. The police officer finally found something to "get" Trevor on after asking him a series of questions about his bike. He impounded Trevor's bike because he was limited to riding it during the day and dusk had fallen. It is not an unusual experience for many African American men to be questioned and psychologically harassed by police officers. What was unique about that day was when a white man, who overheard the harassment, approached Trevor and pressed a twenty-dollar bill in his hands, saying, "Use this to help pay for getting your bike back. I want you to know that not all white people are like him."

Common ground and true friendships will be developed when people of color reject the societal messages that inform us that we are inferior and instead embrace our race as a celebratory aspect of who we are. Likewise, it will only occur when whites reject the privilege and entitlement served to them by that same society and instead embrace a whiteness that transcends modern forms of racism and that allows them to celebrate the gift of whiteness.

"Growing Up with a Race" Journalogue

For Personal Reflection:

What markers tell you about your membership in your race? Biological? (physical features) Cultural? (ways of expression, thinking, and knowing; manner of dress; choice of social activities, language, humor, time orientation) Historical? (how American customs, norms, policies affect you) Physical environment/space? (décor, artwork)

Describe the racial makeup of your family? Social group? Neighborhood? Political circle? Church or faith community?

Have you ever had the experience of racial stress? Racial stress is the psychological discomfort felt based on racial group membership in a situation or particular setting. How did you manage it?

For Group Dialogue:

In what way is your faith community an open door? In what way is it a closed door?

What needs to be acknowledged about race relations in your church community?

For Spiritual Practice:

Acknowledge that God is a master strategist and has created racial diversity as a gift. Graciously receive this gift and acknowledge its presence in your life.

Dealing with Shalita

Struggling to Be the True Self

DURING OUR WALKS, Yvonne follows a number of different routes to get to the same destination. Because I am "directionally challenged," only occasionally do I recognize a few landmarks. However, on these walks I am more concerned with the journey and how long it will take us to get there, and—even more important—how long it will take us to get back from where we actually end up.

While we are getting to whatever destination Yvonne has in mind, we talk a lot about growing up. Not just about *how* we grew up, but about the *process* of growing up. Because we both have been professionally involved with adolescents (I as a former high school teacher and now psychologist, and Yvonne as a former educator and now high school guidance counselor), we have many stories about people in the process of growing up. Often these stories remind us of our adult friends and even of ourselves—all of us still working on the process of growing up. What strikes me about the process is that the journey is so figural that often the destination fades into the background. Developmental psychology affirms this. The key to identity formation is searching and exploration. The journey is more important than the destination.

I like to walk with Yvonne because I enjoy her friendship and our dialogue, and I can walk in peace. I can express my raggedy thoughts and disclose my rough edges. I can talk about my process of growing up. There are other friends that I can do this with—most of them black, some white, and a few Latin, Asian, or Native American Indian. Yet, I find that for most of the folks who have told me about their growing-up process, their stories are rarely shared across racial lines.

First, there is the issue of trust. Myla, a twenty-one-year-old African American college student, shares that this mistrust of white friends starts early. "I had a white friend in kindergarten. We were friends until about age ten; then we never spoke again. All my white friends disappeared around that age. I saw them [whites] as my friends. I don't know if they [whites] ever saw me as a friend. They [whites] didn't need me."

People generally start out trusting others unless they are given a reason not to trust. Unfortunately, for many African Americans, mistrust of whites came early. Just as daily as their morning cereal were negative experiences with whites. Natasha, a twenty-two-year-old African American college student, recalls a white elementary school teacher who said, "You are a lazy group of people." James, a twenty-nine-year-old African American, declares that he does not associate with whites because he doesn't "feel comfortable with people outside of my race. I am uncomfortable with the negative thoughts they [whites] have about us." Victor agrees. "I'd rather have Kool-Aid on my porch with my people."

Middle-aged whites and people of color report that although they can learn to trust one another in the work setting, something happens when they begin to socialize with others outside of their race.

Chris, a forty-something white female graduate student, revealed that she had a fifteen-year friendship with a black woman on the job. They shared their most intimate secrets and got each other through their divorces. Yet, they never socialized outside the work setting. Chris regrets that. She is not sure why socializing outside of work never happened, but she guesses that it had something to do with fear and lack of trust.

Here are the voices of some professional black men on the trust issue:

"They [whites] deal with me in a professional environment. If I come in there with my jeans and t-shirt, they ain't got nothing to say."

"When you socialize with them, you know he is going to call you a nigger when he is drunk, and he is not going to do that in the work environment."

"They don't see you as black in the office, but they don't speak to you when you are at a party or when they see you in the street."

Is it fear, or a lack of diversity competency, that keeps us from crossing those racial lines? If we had mixed-race friends as kids who disappeared in the growing-up process, then we never learned those skills along with all the rest of the adolescent developmental tasks. Thus, as adults, we just don't know what to do when we're around one another outside of work hours.

Until very recently, the racial identity developmental process was excluded from textbooks and courses in developmental psychology. Many pages were devoted to other subjects, and many classroom hours were spent on the topics of physical, cognitive, social, and personality development during all the stages of life. Nothing was ever said about what you do with the visibility of your skin color and how this affects your growing-up process. For most people of color, if they wanted to skip this topic as part of their life experience, it would be impossible. School was always in session.

Shalita is an autobiographical character created by DeWanda Smith Soeder, a graduate of the Diversity Management Program at Cleveland State University. DeWanda, a gifted thespian as well as consultant, chose to create Shalita as part of her thesis research on the use of theater as a diversity intervention tool. Shalita came alive for DeWanda's practicum presentation and her master's thesis oral defense. Imagine, if you will, me in my most professional stance, with my two white, male colleagues, witnessing Shalita and preparing to give feedback on her research:

Shalita, when she emerges out of the adult DeWanda, is about fifteen and she shares with us some of her growing-up process. She is a black, middle-class Southern girl who has a lot of hillbilly in her (the country sharecropping lineage). Her parents try to expose her to all kinds of worldviews through hosting a series of foreign exchange students, some of whom she tries to emulate. She falls in love with Frankie Avalon and Elvis Presley (*them*, not their music) and uses them as her first imaginary boyfriends. She and her little sister play "Beach Blanket Bingo" on their parents' bed. Needless to say, black folks were always wondering if she was "right." In high school, she rebelled by throwing "theme parties." A straight "B" student who had all her graduation credits by the end of eleventh grade, she became sick of black people and their intolerance of her. She chose a predominantly white college—"Hell, I had been a hippy, a vegetarian, meditated regularly, and some of my best friends were white people!"

At the end of her presentation, I was impressed not only by DeWanda's performance but also by the way she had so adeptly illustrated the racial identity confusion that is present for so many adolescents of color. My white colleagues, on the other hand, were impressed that she had managed to get away with cursing in the middle of her thesis defense. Shalita's emergence stupefied me and propelled me back into my own memories of growing up black.

In 1964, when I was a freshman in high school, the Beatles were at their peak of popularity. My friend Gayle from elementary school was really big on the Beatles, and due to her influence, I became a fan as well. Without this Beatles knowledge, I might have had a much rougher time making friends at Notre Dame Academy. As the only black among a sea of white girls, I definitely stood out. Joan approached me. "Do you like the Beatles?" she asked. Thank God that I knew that the correct response to that question was "Yes!" I was in. For a recent Christmas present, I gave Joan the Beatles CD that features their twenty-seven number one hits. Wow! Twenty-seven. Now I know why it was impossible for me to keep up musically. I had to keep the Beatles going for my white friends and all the Motown hits for my black friends.

High school was a challenge to my racial identity process, but I resolved it by being the "race mascot" (a familiar role to many blacks in this situation). I was funny. I made jokes about race. I laughed at their jokes about race. I never confronted. I blended so well that by my junior year I was elected class president and in my senior year was elected vice-president of the student council. At graduation, in the Best and Most ceremonies I was voted "Most Typical '69er," which at that time meant the most representative of the spirit of the class—but in retrospect is quite a joke, considered from a racial perspective!

I went as an observer to my twentieth class reunion. I sat looking at all my former classmates wondering how I had made it through high school sane, while no one else seemed to be struggling with racial identity on top of the basic role-identity confusion. As the struggle of the internal journey that my high school experience and later college and convent experience would send me through, "Getting a good education" suddenly did not seem as important when seen through a twenty-year lens. When I attended the reunion, I thought that the racial identity process was resolved. Yet, while most of my former classmates were concentrating on weight gain and loss, wrinkles, husbands or lack thereof, how many kids, and whether to work outside of the home, I was thinking about race.

The jury is still not in on how we come to terms with our racial identity. What we do know is that the process is complex and perhaps related to life-span developmental tasks. For most whites, the concept of a racial identity rarely surfaces in their daily life. Thus, one's group-membership identity as a white person remains somewhat stable during the course of a lifetime. The face of that white identity does not change in professional or social settings. Many people of color find that a healthy resolution of the racial identity process demands that they have many faces—professional, social, political, and spiritual. For example, being black in each of those contexts may have a totally different meaning. As one black man put it, "I can hardly wait to get home from corporate America and be a black man again."

People of color bump up against the boundary of race more often than do whites, therefore, it is hard to come together to socialize. People of color are rarely off-guard on race issues, especially around whites—even good white friends.

Many of my white friends have shared with me that whites in all-white company do blurt out a number of racially offensive remarks without a second thought. My racially sensitive white friends like Donna spend a great deal of energy "correcting" and "monitoring" these statements. "In a same-race group, people are free to say racist things," Donna says. "Why would I want to say something offensive, if some of my best friends are a member of that race?" It must be frustrating, I imagine, for my white friends who are constantly challenging their own white friends' beliefs. I love them even more for their efforts on behalf of people of color. But it still doesn't make me completely comfortable, knowing that if I leave the room or happen to show up on time, instead of being stereotypically late for a party that I might be stepping on some hidden racial slurs hastily shoved under the carpet.

Because I have spent so much time in the company of white people and understand their culture so well, most whites trust my honesty, my openness, and my ability to see both the hard data (observable, measurable facts) and the soft data (psychological facts) in a situation. I believe even now as a diversity consultant, one of my greatest strengths is really knowing my white audiences well and understanding how whites think.

I know that the vast majority of white people are not racist and are well-intentioned, good people. I also know that the vast majority of white people know very little about what it is like to be black, Asian, Latin, or Native American Indian in the United States and have not given a moment's thought to racial identity issues and concerns. This fact alone makes it difficult to have friends that are of a different race.

My friend Donna, a forty-year-old white health care administrator, says that you have to have a sense of personal security to maintain a mixed-race friendship. Having a friend of a different race requires that "you have an awareness, so that it [racism] can be pointed out to you."
I believe resolving racial identity issues can only happen if you interact and socialize with different races. Otherwise, this very important, visible part of you remains dormant, an undeveloped aspect of your personality. Because of the racial struggle of my high school and convent years, I have a clarity about who I am as a racial being that is undaunted. Now, I am grateful for those experiences and would not trade them.

I became acutely aware of this at my thirtieth class reunion. This time I went as a full participant. I left my husband at home, and Joan and I sped off to see what another ten years had done to the class of '69. This time I was intrigued about stories of kids, careers, and spouse changes, and yes, I still was aware of race. I noticed Kathy, an Asian American woman, who had been in my class the entire time. Since we rarely talked about race except in terms of black/white during the 1960s, I (as well as the others, I imagine) had never seen her as Asian. Maybe she doesn't even identify as Asian (that is the complexity of the racial identity resolution process—you get to claim who you are—ask Tiger Woods). However, I found a weird comfort in fantasizing that there might have been someone else who struggled with race issues during those years at Notre Dame Academy. Kathy and I had a nice conversation that evening. Because I am not completely obsessed with this issue, I didn't yell out to her over the loud music, "So, what was it like for you as a person of color in our class?" but I sure would like to know her answer.

For me, my "Shalita" was firmly embedded during my convent years. In the 1970s, in Catholic religious communities of women, not only did you lose all your material possessions, but your very self was lost—intentionally! Yet, those who were white and whose culture was closer to the historical and psychological roots of the community stood a chance for the survival of self. I did not. I tried it for thirteen years. My leaving was not so much an issue of vocation—I still love the church and am drawn to spiritual growth and practice—but it was impossible for me to survive as a black person in an all-white community (disappointingly, even a religious one). And I even get along well with white people!

What made my survival in a religious community impossible is at the core of what I believe makes it difficult to cross racial lines in friendship. One has to find a way to maintain one's own racial self while at the same time acknowledging and appreciating another person's racial self. You have to be pretty stable in your own racial identity to be able to take in the experience of the other person's racial identity without losing your own. If religious life were culture-free, I might have been able to survive, but it wasn't. St. Patrick's Day was celebrated as if it were a high, holy feast. German customs even influenced how we folded our underwear. Over thirteen years, I ate many meals in the convent and never once was there cornbread and greens (let alone the rice and beans and plantain that I was used to!). And although our liturgies were beautiful, never was a spiritual or gospel song even hummed. But it was even more than the feasts that we celebrated, the customs we followed, the foods that we ate, or the kinds of songs that we sang. White European culture was so embedded in the thinking, values, and ways of knowing in religious life that if I were to continue to live in that environment, I would have no choice but to act like and become a white person. Trying to explain this to some of my religious sisters was like trying to get a fish to understand the concept of wetness. For me, holding on to my black racial identity in religious life would have been like a fish trying to survive outside of water.

I can be friends (and good friends, at that) with white people, but I could not live with them. For many people of color, the boundary is drawn earlier, stopping well short of friendship and socializing with white people. This makes me sad. Just as Yvonne knows many different routes to get to the same destination, surely there must be a way to have friends and socialize across racial lines without one side of the equation losing his or her very self. Maybe if we venture along this new path, one day we may see not only racially diverse religious communities but also a healthier, richer American culture. For now, at least, the journey has to be more figural, in our minds and hearts, than the destination.

"Dealing with Shalita" Journalogue

For Personal Reflection:

What racial stereotypes do you hold (intentionally or unintentionally) that prevent you from crossing racial lines in friendships or socializing?

How figural is your race in your friendships? In cross-racial socializing, do you maintain your racial identity or do you blend into the dominant racial presence?

Has there ever been a time or circumstance that has caused you to struggle with racial identity confusion?

For Group Dialogue:

Describe a situation in which you have lived with a racially-mixed group. What difficulties or challenges were present?

Do you believe it is possible to have an authentically multiracial group experience or does one culture always dominate?

What would an authentically multiracial experience be like?

For Spiritual Practice:

Recognize and acknowledge where you draw the boundary of your racially different friendships. Strive to make this boundary reflective of God's universal love.

FIVE

All Things in Common

Education Leading to Integrated Living

THERE IS A FREEDOM IN WALKING for exercise—especially when you are walking outside. The air seems to freshen the mind, and clarity of thought and expression emerge. When I am walking with Yvonne, she usually speeds up that clarity process by keeping me real. I have translated, "Keeping it real," to mean presenting honesty in the manner one expresses him- or herself. This honesty is derived from actual lived experiences rather than from an experience created in one's head. By now, on these walks, I can sense whether I am being real or not by Yvonne's pace of walking. Yvonne not only walks far but also walks fast. I feel as if I have to walk-run to keep up with her. We negotiated some conditions under which we would walk together—kind of a walking contract after my numerous complaints about her pace. (I got tired of trying to shout at her and she got tired of turning around to reply to me.) One condition was that I would try to speed up and Yvonne agreed to slow down. So when Yvonne starts to return to her natural speed, I know that she has something to say to me but is desperately trying to hold back. Her pace is a signal to me that I need to get a handle on my idealism, that for some reason I am not keeping it real.

Diversity scholars, who have examined communication styles of blacks and whites, characterize blacks as placing a tremendous importance on honesty of expression when communicating, particularly with other members of the race. Whites' communication style, scholars note, are characterized by intellectualization. I translate this to mean that in their conversations words are used to express ideas. These ideas are not necessarily grounded in lived experience, but can merely be lofty thoughts that may or may not be born from lived experience.

Although I am black, I struggle with lofty thought syndrome. In 1980, I believed that racism could be eradicated if people just got to really know one another. My years of living with all-white people in a religious community taught me that if you lived long enough with anyone who was basically good and well intentioned, eventually you would grow to tolerate them. And sometimes you might even grow to appreciate and love them. Surprisingly, you might even find yourself defending them to your own people.

At the time that I was in religious life, we were allowed to return home for a visit only three times a year—never an overnight stay and never for a holiday. I am not sure why we were restricted from the very environment that nurtured the vocation in the first place, but we were. At any rate, many holidays were spent with white folks. On one particular Thanksgiving, I was sitting at the table with a group of nuns with whom I had entered the community on the same day (we called the members of the group we entered with "brothers"—as in the brotherhood of believers would be my guess). I sat across from Sister Mary Valerie. We were months apart in age and we entered the community on the same day. We had kind of an unspoken agreement that we would not make another holiday away from home any more painful than it had to be by trying to drum up meaningless conversation. So we sat in silence over our turkey and mashed potatoes for a while. I actually liked Valerie and was playing the mind game of "how can I make this experience better—who else in the world has it worse than I do, let me think about them" when I looked up at her. I decided to share my thoughts. "Well," I said, "If I have to spend Thanksgiving here, I guess it's not so bad that I have to eat with you." "Yeah, I guess it is not so bad," she agreed. We continued to eat in silence.

During my graduate studies, I found support for my thinking in the empirical studies being done that were based on Gordon Allport's 1954 contact theory of intergroup relations. This theory postulated that racism would be reduced by equal status contact between majority and minority groups in pursuit of common goals. Studies on this theory revealed that whites who had black friends were less likely to say that they preferred to live in an all-white neighborhood and were less likely to believe that whites were more intelligent than blacks. Similarly, studies show that blacks who have more contact with whites grow to appreciate the behaviors of whites and understand their intentions better.

The difficulty in applying the contact theory presents itself in getting people of different races together in the first place. My early experiences, when my family moved to an all-white, rural area, taught me that whites flee from circumstances that would bring them into proximity with blacks (and browns). In 1964, when my nine-member family outgrew our three-bedroom home in the city of Cleveland, my parents decided not to "pioneer any causes" by moving into one of the rapidly integrating suburbs bordering Cleveland. Instead, they decided to build a home on a six-acre lot in the country that they had purchased years before. My parents believed that in that country setting, they could raise us safely, away from urban stress.

My parents taught me that people who espoused racist beliefs were simply ignorant. Our job was to pray for these people. As a result, I grew up thinking that many white people were stupid (ignorant and stupid meant the same thing to me as a child), and I had many white people on my prayer list. When we moved to the country, I added our new next-door neighbors to the list, and prayed hard that they would learn new ways of thinking about us, their new neighbors.

Our next-door neighbors were very angry that blacks had moved not only into town but right next door to them. They immediately erected a barbed-wire fence that stretched the length of our adjoining properties. On each post of the fence, they placed No Trespassing signs. They went so far as to fly a Confederate flag. My sister Eloisa would go to the fence and boldly play a very poor rendition of "Taps" on her trumpet (she was just starting to learn how to play) as they took the flag down each evening.

I was confused about their "ignorance" and fearful of it. My parents, although angry themselves, continued to provide us with security and love, meanwhile teaching us the valuable life-lesson of how to fight racism with dignity. They did everything they needed to do legally and publicly to secure the safety of our family. Politely, yet assertively, they responded to every ploy the community used to get us to move—zoning laws that were suddenly unearthed stating that our land was too narrow for building; school officials who thought my sisters, brother, and I would be better served if we attended another school district where there were already black children (they would graciously see that arrangements could be made); even our Great Dane was cited, for some now-forgotten reason.

Through the course of all of these challenges, my parents led us to believe that they were in charge of not only our family and its space but also the world. They had a great deal of courage and believed strongly that they had a right to live where they pleased. I asked, "Why do these people, who don't even know us, dislike us so much?" My mom's response was that people work hard through their lives to earn the money to buy a nice home. She told me our neighbors had worked really hard to buy their dream home. She had heard from someone that the family had moved "all the way from Euclid [a suburb outside of Cleveland], because blacks were moving into Euclid." Shortly after their move, we came and moved right next door to them. "I guess I would be mad, too, if I were them and felt the way they did!" My mom laughed as she said this, so I knew she was just thinking once again how ignorant some people could be. I prayed extra hard for our neighbors that night.

Despite this experience, I still believed that what I (later) learned as contact theory would work. I also believed in the implosion method—throw the person in the environment for long enough and they will survive and/or have a significant emotional event. There is a great deal of value in diversity education, both in classroom learning (the study and discussion of ideas) and in education through field study (actually going out and experiencing real life). These ideas, applied to diversity management, equal the belief that if you: (1) give people the theory and principles of diversity competency, and (2) expose people to diverse experiences, and eventually, this knowledge and these experiences will influence their thinking and behavior. I was determined to test it out, to prove that these principles work. "All Things in Common" was born.

"All Things in Common" was a group experience in communal living and sharing for young people of diverse backgrounds—race, gender, and class, particularly. The name was derived from the passage in the Acts of the Apostles, where the faithful all live together and own all things in common. I solicited my nun friend, Carol Dikovitsky (then Sister Mary Michael Paul), Father Walt Jenne, and anyone else who was brave and foolish enough to help me. I got some grant money from the Cleveland Diocese and begged the religious community I belonged to at the time for the use of our facilities and buses. As they say, "it must have been meant to be," for no one said no to any of my requests. Twenty-six teens and a group of adult supervisors set out for a full week of simple community living and an experiment in racially-diverse living.

My hypothesis was that if everyone had at least one round of twenty-four/seven in a racially-mixed community, the experience would profoundly affect their lives. It did. What I did not bargain for is how profoundly it would affect mine.

When I was in religious life (another way of saying "when I was a nun"), I focused my energies on social justice issues, particularly in working with black youth, as a way to hold on to my black identity. My apostolate (nun term for assigned ministry or assigned job) was teaching English, psychology, and religion at my alma mater, Notre Dame Academy (NDA). NDA had not changed in its racial makeup since I graduated. In fact, Toni Massey was the new Debbie Plummer, representing the entire black race to that educational environment. It was no mystery to me (and should have been obvious to others) that my work with Black Catholic Input (a diocesan youth group that I founded for black high-school students) and "All Things in Common" were my attempts to put meaning into my world—to make it real.

During the "All Things in Common" week, each day was devoted to a different aspect of social justice and Christian service. Activities were planned so that we would learn about justice, pray together for it, and work together to bring it about. This was a very simple formula. Justice was our common focus. The goal was that we would grow in our understanding and appreciation of one another while living in an isolated environment for a week (no television, phones, or radios allowed).

I have very little natural missionary spirit in the traditional sense of the word, nor am I out to pioneer any causes. I know that my friend, Carol, carried the social justice aspect of the experience for the participants. I can recall spending the day painting houses in the Hough community in inner-city Cleveland with the staff from Fatima Social Service Center (ironically part of my parish community now). The Fatima staff dropped a group of us off with gallons of paint at a home in the area. I, as the adult supervisor, was to lead my group of teens in painting the living and dining room. The only activity I led that day was taking breaks. The teens took over because I was a wreck. I was overwhelmed by the odors—not just the smell of the paint being applied to the walls, but the urine smells from all the little kids running around in the house and the fried food smells that seemed to be permanently in the air. The "All Things in Common" teens, however, did not seem to mind or even notice. They merrily painted as they sang St. Louis Jesuit church songs from memory. Needless to say, the activities of that week were clearly not its highlight for me. The highlight for me was the gift I received in the form of the young participants. Their energy, spirit, and openness on racial issues were tangible. Their insights and willingness to be influenced by one another's realities were profound. After that week, I knew that I would never be able to live again in a community or neighborhood that was not racially diverse.

It has been a little more than twenty years since "All Things in Common." I am still good friends with Sister Carol and Father Jenne, but rarely do I see any of the participants. I wondered whether the week that left them clutching to each other in tears as they said good-bye had any permanent effect on their lives. I telephoned Patty Marshall, now Patty Razzante. Patty, a vibrant white teen from a predominantly white suburb of Cleveland, had not only participated in "All Things in Common" but also had joined Black Catholic Input as one of its few white members. Patty had kept contact with me over the years, and her sister Sue, a head nurse at the time, was instrumental in getting extra support for my dad during his terminal illness. Patty was easy for me to locate, and she was eager to meet for lunch and talk about that week in June of 1980.

Not only did Patty remember the week, but she also had saved and still possessed the original acceptance letter, her reflection notes, the group picture, and other memorabilia. Together we recalled the spirit in which she had embraced social justice issues at the time. She told me that her family life then was so secure that she hadn't given a second thought to entering new and different environments. She admitted that she lost that adventuresome spirit once she had children and became protective of them. Her sources of information on racial issues in America were the media and her work experience. So much of what came from the media was negative, she reported, and unfortunately, her supervisory role in a mental health agency resulted in encounters with some black people who used the race card far too often. She wanted her children to have the same enriching experiences that she had had, but she realizes that she needs to continue to provide a secure environment and be as present to them as her parents were for her. As a single mom, she found that creating such an environment is a constant challenge. She said she knew she needed to get back to her core spirit. She later called and inquired about Cleveland State's Diversity Management Program and has recently graduated with a master's degree and, as a result, has changed her position in her organization to manage its diversity issues. Her enthusiasm for diversity permeates her being and oozes out of her pores. Now, her loving family plays games in which the rules are to intentionally say something culturally insensitive. They take bets on how long it will be before Patty speaks up about it. The one closest to the estimated time wins. It is never more than a minute.

I also spoke with Amy Singleton. Amy was only going into the ninth grade in a predominantly white high school when she attended "All Things in Common." She vividly recalled painting houses and having a picnic with disabled children. Most of all, she remembers the fellowship and the bonding. "Be Not Afraid," a church hymn by a St. Louis Jesuit that was popular at the time, was the week's theme song and whenever the song is sung today in her current parish she thinks of "All Things in Common." The week's experience, she reports, was "very eye-opening." She believes it was the starting point for her interest in social work. She later received a degree in social work and currently works in human resources. She wants to teach her daughters the message that she received that week—that we are all the same in God's eyes. Recently, her first grader brought home some materials from school about Martin Luther King and talked to her mother about that message of racial equality. "I think she's got it," Amy tells me.

Milton Turner is an African American man who teaches Spanish and French at St. Ignatius High School, a Jesuit college prep school in Cleveland. He has taught at St. Ignatius for the past fourteen years. He clearly recalls the service project aspect of the experience—especially because the current students at St. Ignatius are required to complete a service project in their sophomore year. "The week went by so fast. It seems impossible that so many different people of various backgrounds could come together and not be at each other's throats. I've had similar experiences with differences in groups, and that just doesn't happen."

I spoke briefly with Fran, who was sixteen years old at the time she participated in "All Things in Common." "Growing up in the suburbs, I was actually very sheltered. I didn't have a lot of experience meeting other cultures." She continues to experience its impact. "I am very liberal in my thinking and pretty unbiased. It made me more aware of other people." What I learned from Patty—who perhaps had the most intense and enthusiastic response to "All Things in Common" of anyone from the group—and from Amy, Milton, and Fran was that unless the presence of racial diversity is in your face (or on your face, as in the case of people of color) the spirit of "All Things in Common," the message that we are indeed one people with one community, will be lost.

Sometime before "All Things in Common" took place, I went home for a visit. To my surprise (almost shock), I saw my dad was talking to our neighbor. I asked my mother when they had started talking to us. She told me that one morning she and my dad awoke and noticed that someone had taken down the fence. Another day, my dad was out on the riding mower, mowing the lawn. The mower broke just when he had almost completed the task. He struggled unsuccessfully to fix it, gave up trying to do so, and went into the house. A short while later, they looked out the window, only to see our neighbor completing the mowing of the lawn. "He just started being neighborly," she said.

It took almost eight years for our neighbors to become more than just the people whose house was next door to ours. Once they began talking to my family, the friendship between the families soared. At Christmas time, my parents exchanged "To a Good Neighbor" Christmas cards with them. They continued to visit for coffee, share tools, helped with fixing things, and brought over homemade bread and garden-grown vegetables. After twenty-six years of being neighbors, when my parents retired and moved back to the city, there were tears on both sides.

What was responsible for our neighbors' change of heart? We teasingly say that it took them a while to see that we cut our grass, didn't throw chicken bones and watermelon seeds over the fence, and didn't barbecue in the winter on the front porch. We had never spoken a word to them before they started speaking to us, so we reasoned that their original behavior had to come from assumptions and stereotypes. My mom tells me that after spending some time together they were able to talk about— and even laugh about—the early days. Our neighbor told her that he received a lot of pressure from other neighbors to take the fence down. So he took the fence down. Many years after they became friends with my parents, our neighbors also told my parents this story: During one of our family picnics, some of our friends were playing volleyball and the ball went over the fence. Our neighbors' teenage sons refused to give the ball back to our friends. These friends (to this date, we are unsure who they were) went directly to the fence and threatened to burn their house down if they didn't return the ball—and along with returning the ball, they suggested that they "better start being nice to the Plummers, because they are good people." When his sons reported this message to their father, our neighbor later told my parents, that he decided that he "just better start talking." In my opinion, this is just more proof that contact theory works.

In 1997, NBC's *Dateline* televised a special report: "Why Can't We Live Together?" Written and produced by Tom Brokaw, the report tells the story of the affluent city of Matteson, located outside of Chicago. Despite the fact that the blacks moving into Matteson are wealthy professionals, white flight has taken place. City residents have started a campaign to attempt to keep whites in Matteson. In the *Dateline* program, Tom Brokaw interviewed the white residents who stayed in Matteson and those who fled.

I have shown this video many times when I have conducted diversity training. Although I have seen it at least twenty times, it still brings tears to my eyes. My sadness comes because the persons in the report are still so "ignorant." Their perceptions are that when blacks move into a neighborhood, crime increases, property values fall, and school systems decline. They boldly state that these perceptions are "facts." They state that they had to move because their children deserve safe neighborhoods and good schools, and because they need to protect their property investments. Even though Tom Brokaw methodically showed the white residents that there had been a slight increase, not decrease, in property values, that the school test scores remained the same, and that crime did not increase, their perceptions persisted. In their minds, perceptions *are* reality.

Predictably, when I show this video to my diversity-training audiences, many whites find it difficult to believe the message of the video—that racism is responsible for white flight. They tell me that is the way the media chose to present the "facts," and that if the presentation was biased, it must have been because the research was faulty. People of color, in those same audiences, experience a sadness similar to my own. For us, as people of color, this video is proof that racism is still very alive. It is an aspect of modern racism called spatial racism and, unfortunately, persists, beyond former beliefs of racial inferiority.

Spatial racism is a form of racism that depicts a pattern of housing development in which whites create racially and economically segregated suburbs or gentrified areas of the cities. As in the city of Matteson, featured in the *Dateline* special, spatial racism not only happens in lower-class neighborhoods but also can happen in upper middle-class neighborhoods as well. In his 2001 pastoral letter, "Dwell in My Love," Francis Cardinal George, archbishop of Chicago, stated that, "Spatial racism creates a visible chasm between the rich and the poor, and between white people and people of color. It marks a society that contradicts both the

teachings of the Church and our declared national value of opportunity."
In the land of "equal opportunity," I find it hard to believe that some
whites would actually think that for some reason *only* they, as white people, want safe neighborhoods and good school systems for their children,
that somehow they are the *only* ones who want their property values to be
protected, or that for some reason, people of color, especially blacks and
Hispanics, enjoy, or at best are willing to tolerate, crime-ridden neighborhoods, poor schools systems, and worthless property. To me, that kind
of thinking is truly ignorant.

Yet, I still remain an idealist, and I still struggle to put meaning into
my world and keep it real. In recent diversity training sessions that I have
facilitated, participants have added fear to the list of kinds of unintentional, covert racism—another form of modern racism. Ron, a forty-one-
year-old white male states, "We really don't know each other."

In 2004, I find much less "ignorance" in these sessions than I experienced as a facilitator in 1982 and would be met with vigorous challenge by
participants of all races with some of the concepts presented and swallowed
whole even ten years ago. Whites and people of color do challenge one
anothers' assumptions and are willing to confront their fears and move out
of their comfort zones to keep it real. But this takes skill, and these skills do
not automatically come along with good intentions. Here is an example: I
recently attended a gala announcing a new Catholic high school, St. Martin
de Porres in the city of Cleveland. St. Martin de Porres is modeled after
Christo Rey Jesuit High School in Chicago, an enormously successful high
school with a corporate internship program. Students spend one day a week
working at a local business. In return for their work, the businesses agree to
pay a substantial portion of the annual tuition. An enthusiastic group of lay
people, led by Richard Clark, with a great desire to help poor and disad-
vantaged kids, located and purchased a building and raised enough money
to open the school in Fall 2004. As current chair of the advisory board of
St. Thomas Aquinas School (my elementary school alma mater), I accom-
panied Father Mike, Althea Cheatham (principal), and another board
member Joann White to meet with St. Martin's president, Richard Clark. It
was Joann's hope, through her contacts with the Jesuits, that we could get
some helpful advice about restructuring St. Thomas Aquinas, as well as lend
support to Richard Clark as he left his comfortable position as principal of
St. Ignatius High School, a leading Jesuit college prep school in Cleveland,
to begin this new high school for the poor and abandoned.

I wondered, and was joined by Father Mike in my curiosity, what plans and support Richard had in place for moving from an all-white, upper middle-class school to lead a school that would, most undoubtedly, be predominately black, Hispanic, and lower class. Richard passionately explained how on a trip to El Salvador while in a Jesuit chapel he felt called to open this school. We all understood his calling. Father Mike, as a white pastor of a predominately black parish for many years, however, could predict the challenges that Richard was sure to face. Richard candidly and honestly stated that the project was started just as the Jesuits were started—"a group of people, who were friends, got together and wanted to do something good." He then admitted that he had no black friends. At that point, it was confirmed in my mind that he would need a lot of help to keep it real and to turn his "head dreams" into the lived reality of the heart he so desired. To his credit, he is doing the work of moving from good intentions to gaining cultural competence.

My high school alma mater, Notre Dame Academy, is now a coed high school, having merged with Cathedral Latin in the early 1990s. Notre Dame Cathedral Latin (NDCL) remains on the same grounds of my high school escapades with an expanded building and grounds that include a football field. In the summer of 2003, I received a call from the principal to assist her with some concerns she had about the upcoming school year. Sister Margaret Gorman (Peg) is an old friend of mine. Peg is extremely bright and equally as witty. I enjoyed my friendship with her very much when I lived in Chardon. Although I had some unfinished business with NDCL, I was eager to support my friend. She told me that they were expecting six African American students in the fall—a lot for this previously all-white school. She was aware that some unfortunate insensitivities had been made by other students at the freshman "welcoming" orientation and she wanted to put a stop to any other negative interactions. She also wanted to prepare the faculty and own their lack of diversity competency. She requested that I come to the opening faculty meeting to share my experiences of being the "only one" when I was there. I had to remember how to breathe on that request. I promised to think and pray about it over the weekend and get back to her with my answer on Monday.

I decided to do the talk, thinking it was God's way of having me heal from a psychologically painful experience. I know as a psychologist that the ultimate resolution of an issue is when you can take something you have experienced as a suffering and later offer it as a gift to someone else. Starting Black Catholic Input (BCI) had made my experience as a racial minority a gift for me. Yet, it was time to make emotional pain another gift and to receive the gift of their welcoming in return.

I was warmly received by the ninety-member faculty, and I hope they received some insights from my sharing. Another person shared his experience of being a more recent African American graduate. I was so acutely struck by how similar the impact of being the "only one" was of Everett, a 1998 African American graduate, to my own experience of being the "only one" in 1969. I was also acutely aware of the almost tangible energy of good intentions in the room that day of the NDCL faculty. Good, good people with good intentions.

Yet, keeping it real takes work and has to be more than just good intentions. I intentionally choose to keep it real by living in a racially-mixed neighborhood and enjoying social activities where there is a racially-mixed group. Although occasionally I need time to be just with "my people," I know that my life is richer and I feel more alive and real when I am in a setting in which the racial and cultural barriers are removed. I know that this assertion may seem unreal to some people, especially for those whose pace of walking differs from my own, but it is my truth.

My experiences have taught me that when walking partners agree in their contract to keep the same pace, then walking with a similar stride makes it easier to be real. When you are walking at the same pace, you can hear and listen to one another easily. When one group is walking faster and not listening to what the other is saying or has walked so far ahead that they don't even realize that the others are behind them, it is impossible for dialogue to happen. When you are out of sync with your walking companions in life, you will never know when you are not being real.

"All Things in Common" Journalogue

For Personal Reflection:

What recent insights have you had about race relations when talking with a friend, hearing something in the news, or reading something in the newspaper?

How do you intentionally choose to keep it real?

In what way are you still "ignorant"? What perceptions have you made into facts?

For Group Dialogue:

Describe your experiences of contact theory and/or the implosion method for experiencing diversity.

Discuss ways in which you are out of sync with your walking companions in your faith community.

For Spiritual Practice:

Recall a painful experience or a suffering and decide how you can turn it into a gift for someone else.

What If Phil and Kristen Had Come?

The Boundaries of Expression

Most of the time when I walk with Yvonne it is just the two of us. Occasionally her friend Ruby will join us. Yvonne has actually been walking with Ruby longer than she and I have walked together. I like Ruby, but I know that the conversation is different between Yvonne and me when Ruby is present, just as I am sure that the conversation is different when only Yvonne and Ruby are walking together. I admit that I like walking just with Yvonne better—if only because I don't have to edit my words, and Yvonne already knows I have intense thoughts. She always tells me that no one could ever accuse me of having an unexamined life. I use our walks to continue to examine my life and to juxtapose my life against hers and the lives of others that we know. This process is too much and too crazy for anyone else besides Yvonne.

I live in a neighborhood that now prides itself on its racial diversity. Fifty years ago, when this housing development was established, blacks, Jews, and Italians were not allowed. Today, I live comfortably and happily across the street from the Mayers, a very friendly and supportive Jewish family, and next door to the Fragassis whom I consider to be special friends. I have often thought about the fact that fifty years ago, none of us would have experienced the benefits of knowing each other.

Before Phil and Kristen Fragassi had their two sons, Anthony and Mitchell, we socialized often together. Sometimes in racially-mixed settings, sometimes in predominantly white or predominantly black settings, so the race thing is hardly an issue between us. My sister, Felicia, gets a group of friends together every year to celebrate New Year's Eve. She and my brother-in-law love this holiday, so she spends some time searching out the best hotel party—for black people. One year, she invited Phil and Kristen and they agreed to come. Unfortunately, Phil's duties as a physician prevented them from actually attending. During the evening, I found myself seeing what the event would have been like through the lens of white folks. What if Phil and Kristen had come? Would the energy have been different? Would the topics of conversation have changed because whites were present?

I suspect for the group that was present that evening, the tone would not have been radically different. The usual topics would have come up—money, weight gain, politics, and sexual topics from the men—but I know the energy would have been different and there would have been a different flavor of expression. I have witnessed some of my black friends suddenly becoming extreme introverts in the presence of white people. I have witnessed some of my white friends suddenly becoming really stupid in the presence of black people. Strange, indeed.

For my fortieth birthday, I decided to throw my own birthday party. I didn't trust my husband or my friends to come up with something that would work for my myriad friends and I didn't want to burden anybody with that quandary. So, I decided to invite my friends over to our home for food and drinks. First, there was the question of *when* the party should start. I knew that if I started it at 9:00 P.M., my white friends would wonder why I was starting it so late. I knew that if I started it at 7:00 P.M., my friends of color would wonder why I was starting it so early. I set the time for the party at 8:00 P.M. and heard from everybody about what a weird time it was to start a party. "We didn't know if you were going to have dinner or not . . . so I ate" was a common response. Anyway, for about a period of an hour and a half, I had a racially-mixed party (from 9:30 P.M. to 11:00 P.M.). The party became exclusively black after 11:00 P.M. (one black couple arrived when we were cleaning up at 2:00 A.M.).

I believe that folks, no matter what their color, had a good time at the party. During the hour and half of racially-diverse celebrating, no one appeared to be under any tension or strain. Yet, I know that individually both white and black people found it "different" being at my party. Ten years older and wiser, my fiftieth birthday was celebrated at a restaurant with an open invitation to all of my friends beginning "anytime after 7:00 P.M."

A white colleague and good friend of mine, Steve Slane and I conducted a study a few years ago on the subject of racial stress. I defined racial stress as situations or events that are troubling to a person because the circumstances are characterized by acts of discrimination due to race or because the individuals felt their race made the situation harder for them than it was for others. Along with taking a coping-style inventory, we asked respondents to describe racially-stressful experiences. These descriptions were then sorted by content category (relationships, work-related, finances, etc.) and by whether they were active or passive situations. Active situations were those that directly involved the participant, such as being labeled with a racial slur or having a negative trait ascribed to them (such as lazy or stupid), simply because of their racial group membership. Passive situations were those characterized by indirect involvement, such as witnessing an argument between people of different races or feeling intimidated by being the only person of their race in a setting.

Now stop reading this book and think about what our findings were. You guessed it—at least in part. Blacks (our sample of other groups was too small for inclusion) reported more racially-stressful situations than whites, but not by much. Blacks reported 59 percent and whites reported 46 percent. I imagine that the numbers will become more even as the number of minority people increases during this century. Also not surprisingly, blacks reported participating in more active situations (although again not many more) than whites. The vast majority of whites had no racially stressful situation to report. I believe people of color in America are working on changing that.

Steve, my partner in this study, tells a story of his own racially-stressful experience. His car needed servicing and he choose a repair shop that was close to the university where we teach and that had a good reputation. It turned out to be an all-black establishment. This was not a problem for Steve. However, the day that he took his car in for service happened to be the day that the O.J. Simpson verdict was announced; he arrived at the shop just as the verdict was coming across the television. Great timing on Steve's part. He was invited to come to the back of the shop and watch the outcome. There he was—"D White Man"—the only one in the room. He stood in the back behind the others. As the verdict of "Not Guilty" was announced, all heads in the room turned around and all eyes were on him. He simply stood, smiled, shrugged his shoulders, and was smart enough to say NOTHING.

Having "the only one" experience produces stress for all races. People of color just seem to be more "used to it." Whites tend to be fearful. Suzette, a thirty-nine-year-old white female in California, says, "I have had the experience where I have been the only white person in the room and I was fearful. The fear was relatively irrational." At another point, she refers to her confusion about some black cultural references. "I saw these T-shirts with 'It's a Black Thing' on them. I didn't get it. I also wondered about the crown in the back of the car. I saw it five times and all the people were black. What's with the crown?" At the time, I had no special insights on the crown issue. Later, I found out they were air fresheners.

Being understood and understanding the other's race is an issue on both sides. Whites are particularly afraid of messing up and people of color are afraid that whites will mess up. "I want to be able to say things and not be afraid that I will be misunderstood," twenty-one-year-old African American Kila tells me, explaining why she finds it difficult to be friends with whites. "I listen to white people and wait for them to slip up, and I know that is bad."

It is naïve to think that we have overcome racism, although we have entered into discussions—some that have been productive. Yet, in the new millennium, discussions about race, especially between blacks and whites, play out like a movie script. My godson, Paul, is a connoisseur of movie lines. He weaves these lines into his conversation at the appropriate times. If you did not recognize the movie line, you would be struck by the contrast of the words from his usual conversational Ebonics and hip-hop slang. He has seen the movie *Titanic* fifty-one times (imagine those hours!) and can recall a scene from the movie by only music cues. He recites lines from *Titanic* during conversations, and although the line is used appropriately in the conversation, the flow of the conversation is interrupted because the words shift the focus to the movie and not the subject of the conversation.

Race talk in America is like one of these conversations with Paul. Instead of memorized lines from *Titanic,* we have lines that we repeat like this: "If whites were to do this (or say that), it would be labeled racism." "What happened to that white person is wrong, but injustices that happen to black people are way bigger." "Why does it always have to be about race?" "Racism isn't born into somebody, it is learned at home." It is impossible to have a meaningful dialogue on race in America because we are using played-out scripts with lines that have become clichés. Most of us lack the skills and awarenesses necessary to have a productive conversation.

I believe being a "race" is new for white folks and they are trying to understand what their racial group membership means. People of color simply have more experience in this area. Sometimes whites try hard to "get it" about race, but they concentrate too much on everyone else's race rather than on their own. My niece, Mercedes, went to a church retreat with her white friend, Colleen. She laughs, "I knew there were questions and discussion. 'Is she black?' 'We haven't had one in ten years.' 'Hope she's okay with it.' They were extra nice to me. You could tell they were trying to make me feel comfortable."

I have had numerous discussions about race with my white friend, Sally. Sally, of her own accord, has done a lot of personal work on racial identity and instills in her three sons much rich learning about race. What I love about Sally is her ability to be raggedy about it and stay engaged in the process even when she messes up. Here is one such example: As a gift, Sally and her husband Brent gave my husband and me tickets to a play at a newly, restored theater in downtown Cleveland. We include dinner when we get together for events such as plays because Sally and Brent live about fifty miles away from us. These events give us the chance to catch up on one another's lives.

The play was *The Jolson Story.* It was the story of Al Jolson, who was famous for performing in "blackface." The spectacle of white people portraying black people—mispronouncing and stuttering their words, their faces made up to resemble raccoons (symbolizing a "coon," a derogatory term of that time)—was a dominant form of American entertainment for one hundred years. This negative portrayal of black people, by controlling their image, was rooted in an attempt by whites to control blacks.

Both my husband and I knew that Sally and Brent were probably ignorant of the history behind the musical and of its impact on black Americans. We decided to go through with the evening because we enjoy their company, but we would tease them mercilessly when they discovered what the play was about. Sure enough, Sally and Brent arrived at the theater before us and read the playbill. They were already red-faced and apologetic when we got there. We milked it for all it was worth, calling them "Master" all evening and pointing out how very few other black folks there were in the audience. We asked whether our next gift would be a visit to a slave ship.

By the end of the evening, Sally and Brent were able to laugh with us and take their blunder in stride. As I suspected, Sally had been concentrating on the excitement of being at the newly restored theater and had paid very little attention to the content of the play (after all, she reasoned, it must have been good, since it was chosen to kick off the reopening of the theater). The lessons that Sally and Brent learned that evening were far greater than any discomfort Mike and I might have felt about being "the only ones." After all, we are "used to it."

The play, by the way, was tastefully presented—without blackface. The audience was also encouraged to come back later in the season to see *Bring in Da Noise, Bring in Da Funk,* a history of black music in America, and have a discussion about both plays. Sally and Brent invited us to that one as well—and paid for our tickets. Guilt is a wonderful thing!

Friendships exist on different levels. There are friendships that exist primarily on a spiritual/psychological level and some that exist on a behavioral/social level. There are some people with whom we connect spiritually and psychologically and, despite that we may not actually do things with them in a physical sense, we feel a specific bond to them. With those friends, even if you have not seen them for a long time, you can pick up the conversation where you left off as if it were yesterday. Other friendships might occur under different circumstances: you see the friends frequently and engage in a variety of activities together. Some friendships exist on both the spiritual and social levels and these friendships are very special. Friendships that cross racial lines and exist on a spiritual and a social level add a transcendent dimension to our lives.

For me, there is no better example of such a friendship than when I attended the bat mitzvah celebration of the daughter of my friend and trusted colleague, Rich. I shamelessly asked question after question before the event, and Rich was eager to answer them all. I held the date on the calendar as if it were my wedding, I was so excited. My excitement stemmed not only from my friendship with Rich, and my pleasure in the company of his wife, Kennee, who I find has great charm—a kind of down-home spirit combined with sophisticated zest—but also from my anticipation about witnessing a ritual in which past and present were honored in such a way that a vision of the future becomes apparent right before your eyes.

The ceremony was held at Anshe Chesed Fairmount Temple. *Anshe Chesed* translates from Hebrew to "People of Loving Kindness," and the spirit of the day was just that. I had not been in a temple since I had taught sophomore religion classes as a nun over twenty-five years before. Mike, I am sure, had never entered a temple. People were very welcoming and happy to guide us through the experience. Although I had met Rich's thirteen-year-old daughter, Rhoni, on several occasions, I did not really know her. It was hard not to feel "close" to her after that ceremony. She did an amazing job of chanting and interpreting her Haftorah, a section of the Prophetic Books thematically related to the Torah portion. I was especially moved by the honoring of her grandmother, aunts, and uncles as they were called to the *Bima* ("pulpit") for an *Aliyah* ("a chanted blessing"). Rich and Kennee each gave their daughter such a warm, loving tribute that I had to wipe the tears from my eyes.

We had been instructed not to miss the party afterward, for "*they* give really good parties." And a party it was. Kennee and Rich had cleverly arranged to have the kids on one side of the room with a buffet style dinner and the adults on the other side with a sit-down served meal. Since Mike and I were seated at a table right by the dance floor, the divider between the world of teenagers and the world of adults, I began some qualitative research and conducted some participant observations. The white DJ not only spun CDs but also provided entertainment. Joined by a black male and female, who led line dances and illustrated the latest in dance movements, the DJ played the most eclectic array of music I have ever heard at a party. I watched as all the teens, most of whom were from Rhoni's Jewish day school, danced to Sisqo's "Thong Song"—the urban, hip-hop influence was pervasive.

I fell into bed with my feet screaming from all the dancing. Mike, who prides himself on being truly "ghetto"—meaning not only having grown up in the ghetto but also *being* "get-toe," unlike me, who he (and others) believe only grew up *living* in the ghetto—declared, "That was a really *great* time." Always the psychologist, I asked him what made it a great time for him, since I was well aware of what made it so special for me. Besides the really good food, free drinks, and fun dancing, he couldn't say. However, I was acutely aware that he hadn't referred all evening to being "one of a few" or said, "This is so boring, when are we leaving?" So I knew that Rhoni's bat mitzvah celebration had to be something special that transcended race.

The following year, I was invited as a guest speaker to Rhoni's eighth grade class at Agnon School. Their social studies teacher, Mr. Lazur, had introduced a unit on the civil rights movement to the students. He began by asking, "Has Martin Luther King's dream come true?" He encouraged the students to give their honest responses. The class was split fifty/fifty with "yes" and "no" responses. They then studied civil rights history, conducted interviews with African Americans, and conducted a survey with other eighth grade students. I was asked to come and share my response to the question. I prepared my remarks to last about one-half of the allotted time. I was definitely more interested in what the students had to say and wanted to engage them in a dialogue about the topic. They were actively attentive while I shared what the world was like in 1963 when Martin Luther King gave his "I Have a Dream" speech. I gave my response to the question of whether the dream had been fulfilled. In response, a redheaded, green-eyed girl eagerly shared how her experiences with a Puerto Rican friend moved her beyond her sheltered environment. I explained the term "cultural encapsulation." The students readily admitted that their environment was encapsulated. Rhoni shared that when they were given the assignment to interview an African American person, many of them did not know anyone to interview. They were open to change, and they expected this situation to change as they got older. They understood and agreed with me in our dialogue that socializing and crossing racial lines in friendship is a spiritual act. From their responses and expectations, I do not need a crystal ball to predict that for many of the students in that class, this will be an easy and welcomed experience. The banner as you enter Agnon School states its mission—"Teaching Jewish children to think, care and question." There is no doubt in my mind that that is what is happening at Agnon.

In the scripture book of the prophet Isaiah, God gives Israel the title "Chosen Race." Americans tend to focus on the word *race* almost immediately. However, as my pastor, Father Mike, instructs us, it is really the "chosen" part that is most significant. When my husband and I share dinner with Rich and Kennee, Rhoni's parents, we are not only socializing and catching up on the events of one another's lives but also sharing in what it means to be "chosen." We are not a community of chance or happenstance; we are a community of "chosen" people. In choosing a friendship that cuts across differences, we are able to recognize our similarities. Rich and Kennee share with us the impact of the Israeli/Palestinian war and I share with them the impact of being Catholic during the current scandal of sexual abuse of children by priests. We do not solve these problems and perhaps leave with more questions than we came with, but the topics are no longer just words on newsprint or a script of a news anchor. We are a community of chosen people.

In the midst of societal racism, when we can get past the layer of race, even those of different races can be friends and socialize together. It will never happen if we wait until racism is eradicated and people have resolved their racial identity issues. Most people, in the last analysis, are drawn to their friends because of personality. My sister, Nancy, describes her friends as the United Nations. "I am drawn to personality rather than color." Similarly, Louis, who is white says, "I strike a chord with people who have the same likes and dislikes, and it doesn't matter what color. That's what I want for my daughter."

Personality is the unique combination of traits that is the essence of an individual person. Our personality represents our core, our spirit, our soul. Good friendships happen when our core speaks to another's core. This can happen no matter what color a person is. A friendship is a spiritual act. When friendships do cross racial lines, we become open to the transcendent.

"What If Phil and Kristen Had Come?" Journalogue

For Personal Reflection:

Think about your friends. Do they exist on a spiritual or social level or both?

How have your friendships led you to the transcendent?

What boundaries need to be removed to allow the transcendent to be realized?

For Group Dialogue:

Tell how cultural encapsulation is present in your life.

How can we realistically break down barriers to multicultural living?

How can we manage racial stress and discomfort in multicultural settings?

Join the students of Agnon School and respond to the question, has Martin Luther King's dream come true?

For Spiritual Practice:

Consciously and willingly, call forth the presence of God while in a multiracial setting. Doing so is guaranteed to reduce racial stress.

—SEVEN—

What Color Is the Elephant?

Do We Always Have to Talk about Race in Mixed-Race Company?

ALTHOUGH YVONNE AND I have had some pretty intense conversations on our walks, I have never returned home depressed. Even when we are talking about serious topics, we talk about them in a fun way. There is always laughter. I know—because laughter takes a lot of energy and sometimes I have to reserve that energy for trying to walk the distance back home. I have to ask Yvonne to stop making me laugh so that I can keep up with her and get home. Maybe it is the circumstances in which our talks take place, or maybe that when we are walking, we have the illusion that we are getting somewhere, but I never feel weighed down by topics that might normally cause me some discomfort when I am with some other people. Besides exploring taboos, we are also able to talk about the elephants. You can really only talk about elephants safely with trusted friends.

The elephant in the living room is a concept born out of the alcohol-treatment literature. When there is denial even of the existence of an issue or great resistance to talking about something that might be a potential source of conflict, it is like having an elephant in the living room. The elephant is in the living room, but no one is talking about it. We all see it and know it is there, but no one ever talks about it. Some people may even devote their energy and go to great lengths to psychologically cover the elephant up with fancy material, so that people might notice the fabric and not the elephant. My years as a therapist have taught me that elephants are found in more living rooms than just those of alcoholics. Families, organizations, churches, synagogues—they all have their elephants. Where there are human beings, look for elephants. Many people have elephants not only in their living rooms but also in practically every other room in their household.

Certain topics that arise in racially-mixed groups produce the elephant-in-the-living-room effect. After enjoying an evening of particularly lively discussion with an African-American group and then having the same experience the next evening with a white group, I thought it would be good to get both groups together. It only took a moment for me to come to my senses and realize that the energy would never be the same. In fact, members of both groups told me that they would not have felt free to share as they had if members of the other race were in the room. Many people assume that in mixed-race relationships, the subject of race is bound to come up. The topic of race can be unsettling both in a social setting and in interracial friendships. Race, then, in these situations is a big elephant.

We assume a lot from sameness. In the Diversity Management Program, during orientation, I watch the students pair up along racial and ethnic lines. By about mid-year, there is some mixing; and by graduation, the lines are clearly set by personalities. Yet, racial sameness is usually the first selection students make. They assume that the person who shares their racial background also has a similar worldview. "Assumptions," as my husband is always quick to say, can make an "ass out of you and me." Lisa, who is white, is a close friend of my sister, Nancy. At one point in Lisa's career, a large corporation based in Atlanta set out to recruit her. She and her husband were flown from their home in Columbus, Ohio, to Atlanta, Georgia, where they were wined and dined. Lisa spent the day interviewing while her husband did some sightseeing, after which they would rejoin for dinner. Upon sensing that Lisa was seriously considering joining the company, the interviewers decided to share some pointers about housing. "Now you know," they began, "this is Atlanta. There are a lot of *them* down here. But you do not need to worry. They have their places and we have our places." Lisa said nothing, but she enjoyed seeing the looks on their faces when she brought her African American husband to dinner that evening. "Assumptions can make an ass out of you and me."

Although mixed-race friendships are not by any means rare, many people do hold the expectation that their friends will be the same race as they are. Where friendships are concerned, race transcends personality, as well as similarities in occupations and values. Here is a case in point: My husband, Mike, is an engineer—a full-blooded engineer. He is not only employed as an engineer but also lives and thinks like an engineer. Often when we go out with my friends, the occasion is generally loosely planned and somewhat spontaneous. A phone call made that day inquiring about the evening's plans usually gets things started. Mike's friends (fellow engineers), on the other hand, plan events literally months in advance—even if we are just meeting for dinner. Time, place, and confirmed reservations are e-mailed in a precise manner.

One Saturday, we met our friends Julia and Mike for dinner. Mike and I arrived at approximately 7:25 P.M. The reservations were in Julia and Mike's name, and the hostess informed us that they had not yet arrived. Knowing their promptness, we decided to go to the table. We continued to wait for Julia and Mike. I began to get nervous after fifteen minutes since this is equivalent to waiting over an hour for someone in non-engineer land. My husband pulled out his printed e-mail with the confirmed date and place. "Yep," he says, "We are in the right place. Besides, the reservation is in their name, remember?" We asked the waitress again if anyone else was waiting for a couple. "No," she assured us, " *Your* friends are not here." I am convinced, after a half hour that something is dreadfully wrong. I called our voice mail. No message. We inquired again with the waitress, who checked with the hostess; she impatiently comes back to tell us, "We checked. *Your* friends are not here." As she was walking away, I turned to watch her—only to notice the back of Julia's blonde head and the shoulders of Mike, her husband, seated next to her. Not surprisingly, they were being told the same story. Apparently, the restaurant assumed we could not be friends. Now, when I am the first to arrive, I boldly say to people that I am waiting for some friends, and they are white. Hostesses and maître d's always appear a bit taken aback. It might just be that they feel my mention of race is unnecessary—or perhaps they are surprised that I have named the elephant, and they are grateful. "Assumptions make asses out of you and me."

Nobody likes feeling like an ass, so it is time to examine our assumptions about others who are racially different from us. The time for talking about the elephant in our societal living room is long overdue. I am not talking about ugly, evil racist remarks that most people abhor. I am talking about those thoughts in our heads that would cause us to be a bit embarrassed if people were reading our minds. Let's try to stay engaged with one another and not just have the parking-lot discussions after the business meetings or social gatherings. It may keep us from being a bunch of asses.

So many blacks tell me that difficulty in socializing across racial lines persists because whites do not understand black history. Derwin, a black thirty-nine-year-old stockbroker, believes that racial issues remain intense in our country because the problem is a combination of what happened two hundred years ago and what happened in the civil rights movement forty years ago. "They [whites] don't understand our culture and what we have been through as a people."

"I understand what they [blacks] went through—but drop it already. It is in the past." I heard this in another [white] focus group, from Sue and several others. "What about my parents," Louis asks me, "who came here with nothing? They got past it."

Derwin, Sue, and Louis are all about the same age, so they represent a cohort group and have been influenced by the same current events. The zeitgeist, or spirit of the times, would have blown the same currents over all of them. Yet, Derwin, being black, and Sue and Louis, being white, carry contrasting histories that cause them to see the world very differently. Are they likely to be able to work together as professionals? Most definitely. Are they likely to socialize together? Cast your bets.

Let's put the history thing aside for a while and focus on basic communications across racial differences. Let's start with the names we call one another. I've presented many workshops and taught a lot of classes on this topic, so I can identify the hot spots for you. In order to address the "what to call whom, when" dilemma, in many of my workshops, I usually offer a "Lexicon of Appropriate Terms." The lexicon is the research and work of two highly respected diversity consultants, Marilyn Loden and Judith Rosener. I have adapted it over the years, based on responses from the audiences. Generally, before we can get to the specifics of what we appropriately call blacks, Asians, Pacific Islanders, people of Hispanic-Latin American origin, Native American Indians, and white people, there first occurs the, "What is the point of all of this?" discussion. I can usually count on someone to tell me that this is all just a bunch of politically correct garbage. I wait for most of the room to agree with him or her. They usually do. It is generally followed by a "they are so sensitive" discussion, which gets a bunch of head-nods from folks—even from some folks of color. "I don't care what you call me, just don't call me late for dinner" is the weak joke I have heard a thousand times at this point in the workshop. Although predictable, their points are all well taken.

What we call one another does include an element of political correctness. Politics is about the use of power; indeed, what I am called (individually or in my group membership identity) is not only about the name itself but also about *who* has the power to claim that name for me. If I decide that I want to be called Deborah and not Debbie (which I don't, but to make my point), then it is my choice. Similarly, if Asians want to be called Asians and not Orientals (which is an adjective and not a noun—therefore, it does not refer to group of people), then it is their power to do so. Now, I grant you, for novice students of the lexicon, this all might be a bit confusing. "Is it black or African American? I know it's not Negro." "Are they Hispanics or Latinos or Latinas?" "Native Americans or American Indians?" "And why are they offended when I say 'colored people,' when they say 'people of color'? What's the difference?" Since most of us don't have the lexicon memorized or carry around a laminated copy with us in our wallets, here is a simple key to remember what to call people. What we call people is about respect. If my name is Debbie and you call me "out of my name," it can be considered disrespectful. If my racial-group membership identity is African American or black and you prefer to call me Negro because you are fond of that term and the time the term evokes, then it will be considered disrespectful. If you don't know whether I prefer the term black or African American, simply ask. It is a legitimate question, and I am the crazy one if I bop you over the head for asking.

I do not think what we call one another as a group is really all that difficult to master. After all, as Steve, my friend and colleague, is insightful enough to point out, how many times do we actually refer to one another in our racial group membership? We don't walk up to each other and say, "Hi, Debbie, my African American friend."

Let's turn to the "they are so sensitive" point. If I am at a meeting and a colleague that I have been working with for a week suddenly begins to call me Barbara instead of Deborah because the only other person in the room who is black is Barbara, I might just politely correct him and not say anything. If he continues to make the same mistake over and over again, I may choose not to be so polite the next time I correct him. When he tells me not to be so sensitive because we "all look alike," I might choose to take the cover off the elephant.

Another example: I have had many white friends over the years who have said to me at some point in our relationship, "Debbie, I don't think of you as black." There are two aspects to uncovering the elephant in this statement—intention and impact. Undoubtedly, the people who have said this to me have been good friends who have known me for many years. Their intentions, I am sure, were not anywhere in the racist, evil category when they said it. I am relatively sure that in most cases they were trying to give me a "compliment." The impact on me, however, is profound. I will admit I am sensitive about this. I wonder what they do see, if they do not see black. I wonder what being black means to them. I am whirled back into the world of trying to resolve my own racial identity issues and being too white for my black friends and too black for my white friends. Yikes! I immediately feel as if I have been punched in the stomach. Sometimes I want to crawl into a hole, and sometimes I want to punch back. "Gee, she really is sensitive," you might be thinking (if you are white) or "I've been there. I know exactly what you are saying" (if you are a person of color). How do I know this? Inevitably, when I share this example in my training, whites support the intention side and offer me all kinds of ways to understand what my white friend was lovingly trying to say. People of color, particularly other blacks, support the impact side and are eager to have the floor and share their own "I don't think of you as" stories.

Let's move to the other side of the racial fence for a minute, before I come back to the intention-impact model. Often, in the Diversity Management Program, when a white person "gets it" or is considered to have a sensitivity to racial issues that whites are assumed not to have, then people of color claim them as "one of us." The implication here is that when a white person is also affected by something of a racial nature, then he or she isn't really a white person.

My friend and pastor, Father Mike Barth, is a masterful liturgist and preacher. He has an amazing gift of being able to address a sermon to the most motley of audiences—blacks, some whites and Hispanics; old, middle-aged, and teens; GEDs and Ph.Ds.; urban and suburban; ex-convicts and those who have never even received a parking ticket—you name it, we've probably got a representative in our congregation. His message reaches us all, and his style of delivery keeps our attention. He has not only lived in an all-black community more than ten years but also fully embraced the culture and its people. He and my "church sons" share dinner with us on Sundays. Besides trying to influence them spiritually, I work hard to try to instill in Jerome and Paul the universal competencies I feel are necessary for multicultural living—including social etiquette. On the occasion when Father Austin, the General Council of Father Mike's religious order, joined us for dinner, I insisted that they set the table with the good china. "We don't need to use the china, Debbie," Paul chastised me. "Ain't nobody here white but you."

Although I laugh endlessly when they make these remarks, I have to resist the urge to go academic on them. By my count, there were two white persons in the house that day—Father Mike and Father Austin. By Paul's count, there was just me. What I desperately want to communicate to Paul and the many who think like him (not about me being white, but that people like Father Mike and Austin are *not* white) is that they are doing the same thing that people do when they say "Debbie, I don't think of you as black."

"Not exactly," my friends who are people of color might be quick to tell me (there I go being white again!). What whites think about blacks are stereotyped representations perpetuated by the media and a product of their proven racism. When whites say to me, "Debbie, I don't think of you as black," it is because they find it hard to relate positive qualities or intellectual rigor to blacks. What blacks and other racial groups think about whites is based on direct and indirect experiences of being discriminated against. When we think of Father Mike as not being white, it is because our experience of him as a white man is very different from all the other white men we have encountered. I can't argue that those statements aren't true, at least, in part. What I would want to do, however, is examine the assumptions behind them and check out how the persons (white or black) think before I dump them into their basket of racial stereotypes. I realize another fact when I hear these statements. Whites don't really know many blacks, and blacks don't really know many whites.

I have met my share of whites who buy into stereotypical thinking, and I have met a whole lot more who do not. I have also met my share of people of color who hold stereotyped thinking about whites (they are all racist; they are all rich; they all have good credit; they all have clean houses), and I have met a whole lot more who are far more realistic in their views. In mixed-race settings, we need to release the stereotypical views that may have seeped into our consciousness, and we need to learn the skills that will enable us to deal with the elephant in the living room. It is important to take the time to make meaning out of the intention and to unbundle the effects of the impact.

When a white friend says to me, "I don't see you as black," I ask her to explain to me what she means by that. Even closest white friends become uncomfortable with that question. When they get past their own personal discomfort, they usually say something like they do not experience me being anything like all the racist portrayals in the media, or they tell me that I don't resemble what their parents might have said black people were like. Or they admit they're ashamed to be thinking of blacks as poor, uneducated, crafty, and pugnacious, and they acknowledge that they're unclear about where all that comes from (DUH . . .). I express to them the impact on me upon hearing such a statement. And I talk about my personal struggle with racial identity, about what it was like to grow up both black and Catholic (not Baptist) and black and Jamaican-Panamanian (not Southern black). I talk about my experiences in an all-white religious community where there was no room for me to be black, and how I worked to reclaim my black identity. I also talk to them about the joys of being black. All that happens because of just one little statement! It takes time and some skill to understand one another's worldviews. No wonder it is so hard to make friends across racial lines.

Do we always have to talk about race in mixed-race groups? Do people of color always have to bring up the past? A basic lesson that I learned as a therapist applies here. If your patient keeps telling you something that you think has already been answered, maybe it is not because the patient doesn't get it or is being resistant to your therapeutic expertise. Maybe you didn't really *hear* the patient in the first place.

My belief is this: We have to try to really listen to one another, to really hear what the other person is saying and not saying. We have to be willing to hear one another's stories—the intentions and the impact. This, I believe, can happen best in the comfort and security of good friendships. Only in these kinds of relationships will we be able to live in the present and openly discuss the residual effects of the past without creating new wounds.

Now back to whether Derwin, Sue, and Louis could be friends and socialize together. Is your vote in? I vote that they can. I also know that it will require the skill to recognize the elephant and shove it out the door. Not an easy task, but oh, what an accomplishment—and what a relief—when the elephant is finally out of the living room!

"What Color Is the Elephant" Journalogue

For Personal Reflection:

What elephants are in your inner living room?

In your inner world, what are you hearing about your racial beliefs? Is it aligned with God's call for all people to be one?

To whom do you need to listen more carefully?

For Group Dialogue:

How can we create faith communities in which we can openly discuss the residual effects of past racism without creating new wounds?

What elephants are in the living room of your faith community?

What makes it hard in your faith community to discuss racial issues? What would make it easier to move out the elephants?

For Spiritual Practice:

Practice the art of centering by using a mantra or by simply quieting yourself. Centering will help you clarify your intentions so that your impact on others is aligned with your spiritual values.

—EIGHT—

Are We Having Fun Yet?

Leisure-Time Experiences

YVONNE WALKS A LOT MORE THAN I do. I am impressed by how consistent and dedicated she is to walking. When the weather is inclement, she goes to the athletic club to walk. I, on the other hand, am a fair-weather walker. Literally. And even in fair weather, sometimes I choose to go to the athletic club and jump on the treadmill. It is much more structured and time-bound. It gets the exercise over quickly and efficiently. When I choose to walk with Yvonne, it is more of a leisure activity for me. I am doing it more for fun, and the exercise is an added benefit. I really just want to spend some time with my friend, and this is the best way to catch up with her, since she is so busy. Because she is a consistent walker, it is a sure bet that I can book her for this event. When I have fallen off the exercise wagon and I am complaining about my weight, my husband always suggests that I start walking again with Yvonne. "Are you crazy?" I tell him. "Walking with Yvonne for exercise is work. I only walk with her for fun." For Yvonne, I imagine, walking is more of a necessity. She has to do it, she tells me, to stay sane. She does her best thinking when she is walking, and it is one of her favorite forms of exercise. I can see how she says that. I am just glad to be in on what is just fun for me.

It doesn't take much analysis to know that for most Americans leisure time has become a luxury. A weekend is used to run errands: The grocery shopping, dry cleaning, soccer or softball practice, church meetings, all keep us feeling as if we are still working. Vacations are increasingly costly and demand time for planning. A trip to the amusement park or a visit to out-of-town relatives suffices. It is a challenge to find large blocks of time for vacations. It is particularly challenging when you want to share your leisure time with someone else and have to try to coordinate your schedules. I am convinced that my husband spends all of his leisure and vacation time in hour-long chunks at Borders bookstore. Anyone who knows him can count on him hanging out at Borders on weekday evenings and weekends, when he is in town. "It's much better than a bar," is his typical response to my complaints about the time he spends there.

Ironically, although we seem to have less time to devote to leisure activities, we have more choices than ever before about how to spend the little leisure time that we do have. My former director of research, Jeri-Elayne, and I worked on a project assisting a leisure and entertainment institution to increase its patronage by African Americans. We did several African American focus groups on leisure-time activity. Relaxation and having fun topped the list of preferred leisure choices for the focus group participants. When we compared their criteria to what was identified by researchers as "American leisure-choice criteria," relaxation and having fun were nowhere on the list. Well, maybe "feeling comfortable and at ease in one's surroundings" could be translated as relaxation, but it would be a stretch for me to translate any of the other five criteria as "fun" (being with people, social interaction; doing something worthwhile; having a challenge of new experiences; having the opportunity to learn; participating actively).

Fun is a relative term. Hanging out at Borders bookstore reading aerodynamics magazines and drinking coffee is fun for my husband. Not for me (or a lot of other people, I imagine). Thus, the easy answer to the question of why we do not socialize across racial lines is that we have different ideas about what is fun. Maybe, maybe not.

I gave a group of whites and a group of blacks an informal survey on their leisure-time activities. Whites and blacks reported pursuing just about the same leisure activities, and to the same extent: reading, movies, dining out, live theater, sports/games, museums, parks, zoo, jazz clubs, comedy clubs, horse racing, music (listening to it or playing an instrument), roller-skating, water sports, Internet, golfing, shopping, biking, church activities, traveling, and sewing/crafts. Here are the differences: Blacks like going to amusement parks more than whites. Whites enjoy more outdoor nature centers than blacks. Blacks enjoy dancing more than whites. Whites enjoy the arts (painting, pottery) more than blacks. OK, not scientific evidence, but the good news is that we have plenty of things in common that we like to do with our leisure time—more than things that we don't like to do.

My sister Felicia has a counterpoint. "Yes, we do the same leisure activities, but we do them differently. Like music,—we all like to listen to music, but we listen to different music."

Let's check that out. Gosh, darn, my sister was right! At least about the music part. The reported level of enjoyment was about the same for these kinds of music: rock and roll, alternative, reggae, country and western, Latin, and international. Whites and blacks differed significantly on Top 40, classical, big band, classic rock, rhythm and blues, rap (0 percent for whites; 75 percent for blacks), blues, and gospel/religious (11 percent whites, 71 percent blacks), contemporary jazz, modern jazz, and hip-hop (22 percent whites, 82 percent blacks).

This information should not be at all surprising given that difference in music preference is the root of much of the conflict in racially-mixed schools when it comes to homecomings and proms. My niece, Mercedes, and her friend, Meiva, attended their high school's homecoming dance. Jerome and Paul escorted Mercedes, so I heard about it from all sides. All agreed that they had fun but the dance "sucked" because the DJ was terrible. "I barely got to dance at all," Paul complained to me. "They played all pop. The whites liked the DJ and didn't understand it when I said the DJ didn't service blacks," Meiva tells me. "He had it computerized," Mercedes explains. "It [the computer] was hidden over in the corner and most of the blacks didn't even know it was there. I thought the music was OK, but I got sick of 'NSYNC, Backstreet Boys, and Britney Spears. That's all the white kids kept punching in."

This dilemma of universally appreciated entertainment, unfortunately, is not limited just to high school homecoming dances and proms. Organizations struggle with the best ways to acknowledge holidays, and anniversaries and to design employee award programs. Previous to my tenure at Cleveland State University, I was a professional staff member at a liberal arts college. There the tradition of the president's reception kicked off the academic year. What was also a tradition was the way that the black faculty and staff would "make their appearance"—and then go to Burger King for something to eat and on to someone's house for drinks and a real party. On Monday mornings, we had staff meetings. On one particular Monday after the reception, all my colleagues raved about the great time—the music (big band, Top 40) and the food (mostly vegetarian appetizers and gourmet salads) that they thought were fabulous. When it came to discussions about "being a full member of the academic community," minority faculty and staff were generally criticized for not taking part in the many social gatherings hosted at the college. I found myself wondering how many white faculty and staff would come and stay if we served chicken wings and macaroni and cheese and the music was all rap and hip-hop.

If we follow through on Felicia's theory that we do the same things, but do them differently, what do we find, beyond music as leisure-time activity? Yes, all of us read, but are we reading the same books? I have been in several women's book clubs over the years, some predominantly white and others all black. Some of the titles we read did overlap, but clearly the black book clubs sought out and concentrated on black authors or books related to black issues far more often than the white book clubs did. The only exceptions are specifically multicultural book clubs like those sponsored by the Junior League to which I belonged. Because it is a multicultural club, they intentionally selected books of racially diverse interest. It is funny that the club has to be designated as multicultural before we move beyond books by white authors and of white interest.

Yet, even then, "racially diverse" usually means that something is not considered mainstream. Even in bookstores, books by black authors, and any book on race issues, are placed in special sections. As a published author, Ward Connerly criticizes this practice as the "last bastion of segregation in America today." When he went to his local bookstore for a book signing, he discovered that his book had been placed under "African American Interest" as a "service" to the African American community. He reframes this "service" to "disservice" to the general book-buying public and views the "African American Interest" section as the creation of a "red-lined literary ghetto." Relegating books on racial issues or by minority authors to a special shelf not only does economic harm to the authors (robbing them of sales from serendipitous browsing and putting their books at a competitive disadvantage) but also creates "intellectual and cultural damage caused by the bookstore's version of racial profiling." Connerly's book, like most books written by black authors, is intended for readers of any race interested in the subject.

On rare occasions, "racially diverse" can mean mainstream as in the case of The Severance Athletic Club owned and operated by Bill Hawkins. Bill, a white family man with four children, describes himself as a "common-sense thinker." Although he did not grow up in a racially diverse setting, it made good business sense for him to match the culture of his athletic club with the racially-mixed suburb in which the club is located. "It wouldn't make sense for me to hire all twenty-year-old blond girls." Not only does Bill possess good common sense, but his inherent diversity competencies also enable him to make the club work for a diverse population.

When he first started his career in club membership sales, he was often asked by white potential members, "Is this a black club? Is it safe here?" He admits to being perturbed by these remarks. "What does it matter?" he would reply. His club, he has no problems stating, may not be for everyone. It is for any person who is comfortable in racially-diverse settings that bespeaks what America has purported to be—a "melting pot." He believes that every athletic club can provide equipment, fitness trainers, and classes, but "We sell the atmosphere. Here people are just themselves."

The "club" feeling means that all members can experience a homelike atmosphere. It takes work to make all members feel this homelike atmosphere and feel like part of the club. The kind of music to play throughout the club over the loudspeaker presents a particular challenge for Bill. "I tell people to bring a Walkman, but that does not always solve the problem in the weight room, where people can't lift weights easily with a Walkman. I understand that." Bill tries to deal with the symptoms of the problem by alternating music, but he is also looking for more creative ways to manage the diverse tastes that racially-mixed participants bring to a single environment. In the meantime, he spends his time getting to know the members of the club and hiring staff who reflect his belief that diversity provides an opportunity to add value to all groups.

Let's move on to television. Here again, as varied racial groups, we watch television as a form of leisure, but we watch different programs. Go back to my point in the first chapter about *Friends* and *Living Single*. Both programs depict groups of singles living in New York City, but one was the number-one rated show among whites and hardly watched by blacks, and the other was the number-one rated show among blacks and hardly watched by whites. Jim Myers, author of *Afraid of the Dark: What Whites and Blacks Need to Know about Each Other*, suggests that without a crossover in what we view on television, we are literally "tuning each other out." Blacks, for the most part, are used to seeing white culture EVERY-WHERE, so it is not so strange to sit down and watch a television program where people are acting and sounding white. Whites, however, find it strange to watch shows with all-black casts in which people are acting and sounding black. For some whites, it is as if they are watching an international film without dubbed titles. I wonder if people would pause their channel surfing today and watch *The Cosby Show*. At the time *The Cosby Show* moved to its number-one slot, there were far fewer choices for television viewing. If whites today had not taken the time to get past the all-black cast of *The Cosby Show*, they never would have experienced the quality of comedy the show displayed or gotten a glimpse of blacks as professionals, too. Yes, blacks are professionals, and yes, blacks do raise their kids with "mainstream" values and yes, blacks are moral people and on and on. Maybe if whites watched more all-black shows today (unfortunately, much of all TV programming fails to reach the quality of *The Cosby Show*), they would not find the black experience, and by association, people of color groups, so exotic.

This phenomenon is also apparent in movies. The "favorite movie" listing on my informal survey yielded two very different lists for whites and blacks. While the black list contained films like *New Jack City, Do the Right Thing, Boyz n the Hood, Love Jones, Love & Basketball, Soul Food,* and *The Best Man*, not one of these films was on the white list. Is my point to encourage white folks to change their tastes and not identify with white characters and culture in their moviegoing experience? Definitely not. My wish is simply that we all learn how to recognize that there are two sides to a dollar bill. The side that is apparent and obvious to me is only one side. There is another side, just as apparent and obvious to someone else who is also called an American.

Sam Fulwood III, a black editorial journalist with the *Cleveland Plain Dealer*, writes that although he is not a movie critic, he is clearly aware that a movie critique is "merely a reflection of what the reviewer has experienced—or failed to experience—in his life." Failure of experience, Sam Fulwood believes, is the case with two prominent *New York Times* critics who reviewed the movie *Finding Forrester*. Their inability to identify with the black character (as Sam Fulwood can) led them to critique the film as utterly unbelievable Hollywood fantasy. This is an example of ethnocentric thinking. Sure, critics have the right to give their opinion of the film—that's their job. But I am continually amazed that white journalists, politicians, and writers get to define what is real and what is the American experience. At least they should have the intellectual integrity to be able to acknowledge that their statements only reflect one worldview. Maybe these professionals just don't know that.

My consulting experience has heightened my awareness that what may seem so obvious to me as a person of color may be new information to those of the majority race. In one organization, I was contracted to assist with their retention of minority employees. Because the morale was generally good and the compensation package generous, the organization was at a loss to understand why they had difficulty retaining talented people of color. The answer was relatively simple. Although the organization was far from discriminatory in practice, it had done little to integrate and utilize the full potential of their minority employees. One African American woman reported to me that she was given the "employee of the month" award for her service record. She laughed as she shared with me that her "reward" was a gift certificate to a tanning salon. "Obviously, they didn't expect me to be given this award," she said.

Progressive organizations are engaging in diversity efforts not only to avoid lawsuits but also to remain competitive and actually increase their revenues. Building inclusive work environments is synonymous with managing diversity. Yet, you can't give what you don't have. It is a difficult task to build inclusive environments. Anyone would be at a loss to know how to be inclusive if his or her entire life were singularly focused on same-race experiences. I am convinced that all the executive coaching on diversity I do would virtually disappear if each one of those white executives just had a good friend of color and each black executive had a good white friend. Moreover, I am not talking about just a trusted coworker of another race, I mean a real friend with whom one socializes outside company walls.

If you are a white executive and you have a black (Latino, Asian, or Native American Indian) friend, you are less likely to think about minority employees as unable to be promoted. It will be easier to see people of color as team players, mentees, and possibly the next president of the company. If you have a white friend and you are a black executive and you have white people above and below you, you are less likely to think of them as racist or disrespectful. You may be less likely to question their motives and interpret their actions as destructive. Career advancement—for whites and people of color—is often based on a broad range of experience beyond functional expertise. Studies have shown that successful executives build genuine, close personal relationships with both whites and people of color.

Of the twenty-six million new workers coming into the workforce by 2005, 40 percent are expected to be people of color. Getting along in the office is based on how we get along outside of the office. In addition to all the diversity interventions taking place in organizations, we need to search for ways to enjoy one another outside the office.

"I grew up in the northwest side of Chicago—all lily-white," Marianne tells me. "I started working and taking hold of black friends. They were real and grounded. They would look at me and would say, 'You're nuts.' That's what I love about black culture. They make you see it the way it is. They are more open." I am not saying that Marianne's experience of black friends will necessarily be everyone's experience. My point is that she was aware of "the other side of the dollar bill" because of her friendships that crossed racial lines. Her outlook on life and her work perspective were enhanced. In today's increasingly multiracial market, that is a necessary competency.

Let's get back to our leisure-time activity comparison analysis. We are all dining out, but we go to different restaurants—or to the same restaurants at different times. We go to comedy clubs—but to hear different comedians. We attend plays, museums, parks, and zoos, but we do so in segregated groups. We have different ideas about what is fun and what is considered funny.

My two nieces, Mercedes and Leslie, live in the same city as I do, so I see a lot more of them than I do of my other two nieces. I have had the privilege of being part of their lives and have had the opportunity to witness their growing up. As they entered their teenage years, all the typical behaviors of teens came right along—just as if they were case studies from a textbook. I witness the same phenomena for Jerome and Paul. Hanging out with me is no longer cool; what I request from them has a literal price tag on it for them even to consider the suggestion, let alone carry it out; I no longer know anything, and what little I may know is not at all relevant. You get it, and most likely you have experienced it.

I also have watched them becoming increasingly funny. I mean being really witty. They have the ability to see life in such a real and vibrant way. Life is funny to them, and as a result, they are funny. As a serious adult, I know that I have to work hard to stay a part of their world. Otherwise, I would not appreciate their view of life or their humor. Instead, I would only see them as the strange human beings I know that they sometimes are.

Their parents and the other adults in their lives are witnessing this manifestation of life-stage development, and they talk a lot about it as well. When we are not trying to keep our cool about something the teens have done, we are laughing at them and with them. When I see Father Mike buying a hip-hop CD for himself, I know that it is not just because he has been exposed to their music (constantly), understands what it is about, and can appreciate it (certain aspects). I know that listening to hip-hop is another way he stays connected to their world.

Staying the course with our teens is critical. Many parents lose them at this stage by mistakenly becoming less involved in their lives, instead of differently involved. Similarly, if we as Americans continue this racial segregation of our social lives, we will grow further and further apart. Socializing across racial lines requires no more effort than the effort that it takes to stay engaged with our teenaged loved ones. The other race may appear to be a bit strange at first, but with time, we will learn to experience our time together as fun and to appreciate other people's experience of life as funny.

"Are We Having Fun Yet?" Journalogue

For Personal Reflection:

What circumstances allow you to feel at home? How race-specific are those circumstances?

What is your definition of fun? In group activities, does fun decrease or increase in racially-mixed groups?

For Group Dialogue:

What characteristics of your faith community support inclusion?

What is the "other side of the dollar bill" that you wish others in your faith community could see?

Share your experience of a great leisure activity and note the similarities and differences.

For Spiritual Practice:

Be open and willing to receive the goodness of life by a multiracial leisure activity. If your faith community is monoracial, consider intentionally planning and executing an inclusive social activity with another community.

—NINE—

Gentle Bumping

Supports and Barriers to Cross-Racial Socializing

I HAVE NEVER KNOWN A TIME during my walks with Yvonne when one of us is not talking. It is not that we do not value silence, but rather that one of the primary reasons we walk together is so that we will have time to talk. Although subjects range from family to work to church life, occasionally we discuss controversial topics. I think because we share the same spiritual base we disagree on very few topics. I believe, however, that I am much more liberal in my thinking than Yvonne is. In practice and behavior, I am rather conservative, so our behaviors tend to be similar since they arise from the same value base. Because Yvonne knows my actions, I am comfortable bringing up as many controversial topics as my liberal mind will let me, and Yvonne knows that I am just talking. My "what ifs" and "supposes" lead me to broaden my thinking and once the thought is there, then the possibility for its accompanying action exists. I find that Yvonne's response to my bantering provides a wonderful balance between challenge and support. At the juncture of challenge and support, growth happens. Good friends that challenge as well as support us contribute enormously to our development.

Friendships, like people, have a developmental pattern. In early childhood, we form our friends based on geography. We become friends with others in the neighborhood or the kids of our parents' friends; or friends come from our church, synagogue, or mosque. In late childhood, friendships are based on sharing particular activities—sports, clubs, learning the same musical instrument. In adolescence, friendships are based on emotional support and serve as a testing ground for new values and working out our identity. In adulthood, friendships are based on shared values, attitudes, and expectations. In later adulthood, friendships provide considerable stability and life satisfaction.

Very few people would doubt the value friendships add to our lives. Outside of family, friends provide the primary vehicle for support. Some people, however, might question the benefit that cross-racial friendships provide. The value of cross-racial friendships is that they provide us with a maximum vehicle for self-expression. We increase our chances of being fully authentic by bumping up against differences. Bumping up against differences helps us define who we are. Cross-racial friendships provide gentle bumping.

Dee West, a professional black woman in a college setting, shares with me her experience of gentle bumping.

My closest friend is a white male whom I am in communication with on a regular basis (e.g., he lives in Connecticut so we talk on the phone at least once a week and communicate by e-mail almost daily). He and I met in the workplace—around the time of the LA riots—immediately following a staff meeting. In fact, I was a bit surprised that he actually approached me because as a new staff member he had described himself as rather politically conservative and, based on some of his right-winged comments, I thought that his approach would be quite separatist. When we worked together, I was the only African American on staff so I was certain that he and I would spend little if any "non-work-related" time together. However, as time progressed, he sought me more out for social reasons. In his own words, he expressed that he found me "intriguing," "different," and all of the typical "you don't meet my stereotypes of a black woman" stuff. Ironically, following that somewhat ignorant icebreaker, we became fast friends. I had thought to myself "at least he's honest." When he said to me that I was "intriguing," I actually knew what he meant but pressed him to talk more about it. In the most particular way he said, "Well, when you said that you felt that O.J. Simpson was probably guilty, it surprised me. . . . I thought all black people thought he was innocent." In essence, this strange white man had latched on to me because I obviously came across as somewhat sage, or for lack of better words, a "good black." To date, he and I have great debates about everything in life from race to politics. However, MOST of our conversations are about race. In fact, we share our divergent views openly and freely, almost to the point of inflicting pain upon one another.

In Dee's latest conversation with her friend, she reports to me that he seemed quite taken aback when "I answered my telephone with an Islamic greeting 'As Salaamu Alaikum.' What he hadn't known at the time was that, for personal enrichment, I am studying Islam and Arabic. I hadn't shared this with him because he is staunchly patriotic (America is the mecca and white Americans can do no wrong) and, based on some of our conversations, it is clear that he would have resorted to acute ethnocentrism. Anyway, the simple greeting turned into a two-hour talk about militant blacks, angry blacks, etc. . . . Although we laughed, argued, resorted to silence, etc., . . . we ended the conversation with 'I love you' as we always do. Although there are many cultural differences between us, what really drives our friendship is the sincere attempts at honesty between us. He and I create for one another a space to talk openly, across racial taboos and about our deep frustrations about race. Our friendship is a beautiful one though because we both fight and love vigorously."

There are others with whom Dee reports she has less intense relationships; other white friends whom she loves just as much, yet they never discuss race matters. Why? She states:

Perhaps it is because their interest is in other areas or what brought us together had to do with things other than the fact that we are white, black, whatever. Perhaps because I'm not, as in the case with Wes [her friend previously described], their first "real black friend" so the incessant need to test the racial waters is not a priority. However, in those cases, connection is, on the surface, less political, but there is always, at least on my part, an awareness that racial differences exist. For example, going into a restaurant or other public place with a white male friend still gets stares or odd looks from others. I am aware of that, and now that I've pointed it out to the white men in my life, so are they. These kinds of "awarenesses" are often shocking to them, but like everything else, we analyze and discuss.

The other day one of my white men (I jokingly call them that) told me he wanted to experience the black church and he wanted to go to church with me. I said "you don't realize how fortunate you are to have

me . . . If it weren't for me, you'd just be curious like the rest of them."
We laughed our knowing laugh. We both know that, although we care
about one another, our friendship is as much about a "diversity experience" as it is about love. However, we realize that society did this to us,
so we keep loving and keep coping.

Others, like Dee, state that their friendships with friends who are
racially different from them often include intense discussions about race.
Faye, a fifty-five-year-old African American woman, has enjoyed for many
years a friendship with Donna, who is white. She describes Donna as a
sister. Like sisters, they have disagreements, particularly when it comes to
racial matters. They both enjoy dancing and often go to black clubs.
Because Donna's world has included blacks for so long, she will render an
opinion on a racial subject. Faye believes that her experience is "valid
because I am black and grew up with this attitude" and has witnessed it
among her black friends. "I thought it odd that she [Donna] thought she
knew more about being black than I did." Yet, she reports no discomfort
from their disagreements. Faye believes Donna retains her white identity
despite her many black friends and she is able to retain her black identity while socializing in Donna's world.

Yet, for many people any kind of bumping experience—even gentle
bumping—evokes resistance. Thirty-five-year-old Yvette believes, "Whites
have to be pushed to move into other cultures." She may have a point.
However, resistance to cross-racial socializing is not just from whites but
also from many people of color. Larry, a thirty-two-year-old African
American financial planner recalls a bad experience in his Catholic elementary school. As an eleven-year-old, he vividly remembers a nun using
the rhyme, "Eenie, meanie, minie, mo, catch a nigger by his toes," to
choose which student would go to the board. Since that time he reports he
"keeps them [whites] at arm's length until they prove themselves to me."

As a change management consultant, I know that resistance is natural
response to many human experiences. My training in Gestalt theory has
taught me that resistance is merely information about the resister's thinking
and values. When perceived through this lens, resistance is a useful tool for
facilitating change. In cross-racial interactions, listening to one another's life
stories helps us understand resistance and build healthy friendships.

Our families, educational systems, work environments, church, synagogue, and mosque communities can act as either supports to eliminating

resistance to racial diversity and creating cross-race friendships or barriers by maintaining and sometimes creating resistance to these friendships.

To unravel the web that is often created by these systems when they have become barriers is indeed quite a task. Any behavioral change process requires that the person or system first experience a high enough degree of dissatisfaction with the current state to want to change. Then they have to have some kind of vision or mental image of what the desired state might look like. Then, they have to possess the skill sets necessary to make that change happen. This is how resistance to change gets broken down.

I believe as a nation we have done a lot of visioning about what a world would look like without racial boundaries. Martin Luther King's dream speech is frequently quoted and supported in theory by blacks, other people of color, and whites. We do well with visioning. In my opinion, most of us lack dissatisfaction with the current monoracial environments that we have created and most of us lack the necessary skills to interact successfully across racial lines. Thus, we spend most of our energies resisting cross-racial interactions. We need to start first with managing the resistance.

Understanding is a first step to managing resistance. Recognizing some area of common ground facilitates understanding. For many blacks, the common ground is easily recognized with other people of color. James, a thirty-year-old black man states, "I can relate more to Hispanics than to whites. They have the same mindset. It is also easier for me with Jewish people because we have a shared history of discrimination."

Elizabeth, a young white woman, states that her experiences growing up as one of few whites in a predominately black school has often put her in the role of the "human racial translator." In high school, she had a friend who introduced her to a new girl who was black. When Dacia got to me, she said, "This is Liz, don't mess with her; she is the blackest white girl you will ever meet." Upon hearing this, I looked up from my work so confused on what that meant. I mean, I never purposely "acted black" or "dressed black" like some white girls did, I always just acted like myself. I am sure I was influenced by my environment some, but being or acting "black" was never a conscious act. After hearing this, I sat back and assessed what I knew about African Americans and I found that I knew a lot more than many white girls would know. . . . When I went to college, I found my experiences were helpful in the big picture of life. I made lots of friends of all colors and walks of life, and thought I felt most comfortable around African American people.

Later, she reports, in many late-night talks with racially mixed groups of friends, an African American friend, Robyn, taught her she should "be proud of what color I am and who I am and where I came from because that is what made me who I am today."

For most people, the common ground of work has provided them with the opportunity to cross racial lines. Some persons report that because of their work environment they are more open to people of different races. As a thirty-five-year-old black computer analyst, Aaron believes this to be true. "Workplace has become the only place to learn about races. I work in a white setting. We have roundtable discussions and people look at me and say, 'What do you think?'" Aaron feels the learning is bidirectional—whites learn about him as a black man and he learns about them as whites.

Neisha, an African American woman has been in corporate America all of her professional life. She talks about the friendships she has made that cross racial lines:

> They consist of Latino(a) and white. One of the most significant ones is a white female that I met in 1982. We have supported each other with children, parents, siblings, ex-husbands, and deaths. We have traveled together to transport her daughter to spend shared time with her ex-husband. I was able to lend her emotional support/encouragement during the time her current husband was fired with other air traffic controllers, the death of her sister, a drug problem with her daughter and the divorce of her son. I gave a character witness interview for her. Every city (five) that they have relocated to over the years, I have visited and spent the weekend at their home. Last year I attended her husband's retirement ceremony to witness both of them getting pinned with honors. She was very supportive to me when I was facing the trials and tribulations of my son, the near-death experience with my daughter and most recently, the death of my dad.

As a Marine, Eric, a thirty-three-year-old small-business owner in California, learned about racial differences. "When people are forced to cross racial lines, you learn there is no color except green. You end up with people you would not normally be around."

Getting beyond the fear of making mistakes in cross-racial groups and learning to live with some emotional discomfort are bumps to be ridden over on the journey of meaningful cross-racial friendships. Marlene, a forty-something white, Jewish woman states,

I have frequently fallen into the trap of assuming that because I have a friendship with one black female, for example, all black females will want a similar relationship. I just bumped up against that again in my new job. I have an African American woman who reports to me. Fortunately, a trusted friend and colleague cautioned me about the way I was talking about our pending relationship and caused me to reconsider my approach.

Marlene now knows that the path she needs to embark on is a journey of learning about her own history—white history. "Not revisionist versions, but real history." She tells me, "I can forget that this is a journey that will only be finished when I am dead. I can't let my fear of 'being called a racist' get in the way of being as authentic as possible in those relationships I do have—bearing in mind that my intent and impact may not always be the same."

Ann, a forty-something African American administrator in a university, relays the challenge of cross-racial friendships this way:

For me, personally, it has been challenging having friends of another race. I have a friend who was my next-door neighbor at one time. We were close then, however, she moved and I also moved, and now the friendship is more like an acquaintance. The challenges seemed to arise most often during social occasions. I wasn't comfortable with her family and friends and could sense that some of my family and friends weren't always comfortable with her. When she first moved, she called a lot about getting together, but I noticed that when my family and friends visited we were the only visitors. I wondered why we weren't invited to things that involved other family and friends anymore. We were invited to her son's bar mitzvah and I observed that we were the only African-Americans there. We talk every now and then and occasionally get together, but it is more like an acquaintance relationship. I have other cross-racial acquaintances and colleagues, but we only socialize at work related functions.

One can hope common ground can be found as a basis for cross-racial friendships in other ways beyond working side by side. One need not be the world's biggest risk-taker to gain a friend of a different race.

Stephanie, a thirty-three-year-old black analyst shares her experience with me of meeting her first white friend. "I grew up with all blacks and have always been a loner. It was through talking about the book *Memoirs of a Geisha* that I ended up bonding with a white woman who is now a good friend."

When we closely examine our resistances, we can experience that freedom of thought can lead to changed behavior. Crossing racial lines in friendships requires the courage of knowing oneself and having a vision of a world without racial boundaries. Knowing oneself is a developmental process. Good friends, especially those that cross racial lines, expand our self boundaries in ways that we could never imagine. Most of us are bigger and better than we believe ourselves to be. We learn that in these friendships.

"Gentle Bumping" Journalogue

For Personal Reflection:

How have cross-racial friendships expanded your sense of self? How has this enhanced your spiritual identity?

What are your personal resistances to crossing racial lines in friendships outside of work settings?

For Group Dialogue:

Listen to one anothers' stories about cross-racial socializing as a way to break down resistance.

Share your vision of a world without racial boundaries. Compare that vision to the stated principles of your faith community.

For Spiritual Practice:

Examine the ways God had made your race significant or insignificant in your life. Intentionally choose to create a world without racial boundaries and enhance the gift of your racial identity and racial diversity.

—T E N—

Some of My Best Friends Are . . .

Positive Changes for Multiracial Living

WHEN I WALK WITH YVONNE, we walk without a destination; we are simply walking and talking. On the occasional walk with my white friends, we have a destination. Kristen and I used to walk to Weight Watchers meetings. However, when summer became autumn and we had too many TLB's (Weight Watcher language for tastes, licks, and bites) that week and were too fearful to weigh-in, we stopped walking! Jo and I used to walk to Dairy Queen to "make up for" calories contained in the Blizzard and Peanut Buster Parfaits we were going to devour. When I review the origins of my friendship list, it appears that my friends who are white are former classmates or are current or former colleagues or co-workers. My black friendships have originated from social gatherings or in meetings of social organizations. I met Yvonne at an athletic club in a step-aerobic class, and we have been close friends since that time. As I explore the topic of cross-racial friendships and socializing, it has caused me to examine if I step differently with my white friends than I do with my black friends and why that might be so.

I remember sitting on the steps of our house one summer day when I was about seven or eight. I was playing with Shelley, Toni, and "them" ("them" changed—Shelley and Toni were the core). We would call out the familiar rhyme of "So-and-So and So-and-So sitting in a tree, K-I-S-S-I-N-G. First comes love, then comes marriage, then comes So-and-So with the baby carriage." We would fill in the names with kids from the neighborhood and from school. Once, my sister Eloisa (even then pretty whacked) named a black/white combination. I remember the hush and then "Oooohhh." We stopped singing, shocked, feeling as if we had just been caught cursing.

Many contend that the fear of socializing across racial lines is rooted in the taboo against interracial dating and marriage. Perhaps that taboo is why the races seem to separate socially around junior high school. Negative attitudes toward interracial dating have indeed changed over the years, and most persons are either much more tolerant of, or remain neutral about, interracial couples than ever before. Yet there are more than a few "sistahs" who sizzle when they see black men with white women, or who resist vehemently when I urge them in therapy to widen their pool of candidates for potential mates to include white men. White men are still accused of getting themselves a "jungle bunny" when they cross the racial line with women of color. A white man in his late twenties who is married to a black woman told me during a recent diversity-training session, he is constantly expected to justify his choice for a partner, and his wife repeatedly has to explain her choice.

As an adolescent growing up in the 1960s, who imbibed the spirit of the black power movement and was nourished on the civil-rights zeitgeist, I have had to grow into my acceptance of interracial marriages. My brother, Paul, married a white Swedish woman, Bettina, and although most times I favored Bettina's line of thinking over my brother's ideas, I still held the position that black men should marry black women. At the time that I left the convent and began looking for a mate, I cared much more about what other people thought about my life choices. My fear about marrying a white man was based solely on my fear that others would interpret my choice of a white partner as a statement about my weak or nonexistent affiliation with blacks. I was actually listening to the voice of my own insecure African American racial identity. Today, if I were looking for a mate and not already happy with the "brotha" I got, I would think differently about white men as potential mates. Having resolved my own racial identity issues, I would not let racial lines be a barrier to a loving relationship.

A white male friend who challenged my beliefs on this topic caused me to pause and rethink my position. I reasoned that there would be days when I would come home and would not want to talk with a white partner, simply because he was white. I didn't know how the relationship could survive on the days of "had too much white people." He asked, "Well, aren't there times when you just don't want to talk to Mike [my husband]? How would that be different?" He was right. I thought about how often I have lumped Mike into the "He can't help it, he's male category" in order to let go of something he has said or done. Those feelings have not rocked our marriage or my love for him. Would it really be any different with a white guy?

A conversation on the same topic with my friend Herb, who is Native American Indian, also enlightened my world of racially inconsistent thinking. He pointed out that my ruling him out as a potential mate [if both of us were not married and were seeking partners] simply because of his race, was as hurtful to him as any other racially exclusive actions. I could choose to rule him out for other reasons related to personality or preference, but to do so simply because of his skin color was absurd. I had to agree.

We have much to learn from those persons who have not only crossed racial lines in friendship but also pushed the boundary to marriage. I did so, sharing Chinese food and conversation with a group of interracial married couples whose stories speak to our common humanity. They were all friends of many years and had achieved, unconsciously, a kind of support group for one another. The themes of having a strong family of origin, unwavering faith, a firm educational foundation, and exposure to multicultural experiences, permeated the evening's conversation. None of them had planned to marry someone black or white. Although there was some discomfort and fear during the initial stages of their relationships, none of them were rejected by their families. All of them had been raised in churchgoing families.

Ultimately, their choice of marriage partners came down to an issue of trust on the part of those who knew them. Eric states, "I was going to a private school and had my first white girlfriend. My parents had always told me that it didn't matter who I brought into the house. They knew that I was a good person, and therefore that person had to be a good person."

Patti stated that her parents decided that they had "raised me and did their best. It was my decision."

Another Eric in the group shared similar parental responses. "They understood that they put me in a certain setting where interracial dating was a possibility. I got the message that 'Eric, we would prefer . . . but if you do, it will be tough on you, but we will always support you.'"

Carlton and Kelly recalled that her mom's limited encounters with blacks were a source of her initial discomfort with their relationship. However, once her stereotypical perceptions were erased, their interracial marriage was never an issue.

Perceptions drive much of the fear that underlies socializing across racial lines and thus interracial dating and marriage as well. All the racial ghosts come out of the closet when two people—one white, one black—want to get together.

Many parents drive home the message born of this perception early in their children's lives. Andrew, a professional black man in one focus group, candidly expressed his concerns about the possibility that his young son might date a white woman. "I'll tell him that it is alright for now to be friends, but after a time, if he is still looking at little white Suzy over here, he's going to know that he needs to be talking to Shaneequa." Apparently, any black Shaneequa, in his mind, would cause a lot less hassle in his life than any white Suzy.

On the other side of the racial fence, Mary Ellen reveals that "My father was not a prejudiced person, but the message was clear—DO NOT bring a black boy into this house. The preference was strong—if he were Catholic, and especially Catholic and Slovenian, then there would be a big wedding."

Interestingly enough, thirty-nine-year-old Mary Ellen also told me that, although she and her husband are both white and Catholic, she is the only one of her six siblings who entered into such a union. Several interracial and interfaith marriages exist in her family (Puerto Rican, Jehovah Witness, Jewish, and Vietnamese atheist). "Yet we are all the same, as married couples. Have the same problems. Same conflicts."

All the interracial couples that I spoke with have encountered concerns expressed by family and friends—especially concerning children—but they had not experienced direct or indirect sanctions against dating or marrying someone of a different race. As a young, upwardly mobile group, they didn't seem to be fazed by the task of raising biracial children. "There are so many differences in the world, what is one more difference?" thirty-two-year-old Korine asks. Simply put. I wish we could be living that simply.

At the risk of oversimplifying the issue, I believe that interracial couples support us all in moving toward a shared American experience. In my diversity-training sessions, we often progress toward an animated discussion about what exactly is the American experience. All of our ancestors, except for those of Native American Indians, arrived in this country by boat—the difference is in the kind of boat. Some were cruise ships and some were slave ships. The American Dream, that anyone may create a "rags to riches" success, has historically been a nightmare for some racial groups. Similarly, the "bootstrap" theory—that anyone can succeed through diligence and hard work ("pulling oneself up by one's boot-straps")—only applies to those who have boots and, more particularly, boots with straps. From this perspective, the historical background of your racial heritage frames your relationship to America and thus dictates the kind of American experience you might have. What I witness in inter-racial couples is not only the ability to disencumber themselves of soci-ety's racial baggage but also evidence of the inherent God-given right that each of us has to fulfill our human potential by loving. It is how we love, not our historical relationship to America, that dictates our ability to grasp the richness of the American experience. Yes, we are really free to love in America.

Yet, as a psychologist, I know that, on an individual level, when some-one's history has been marked by abuse and neglect, or steeped in the material poverty that prevents one's progress, it takes a great deal of time to heal the wounds and form a relationship with the abuser. Often, these persons find it difficult or impossible to love until the unfinished work of their past has been psychologically completed. Similarly, for many people of color, on a societal level, this is the case with their relationship with America. We, as racial minorities, focus on how far we still have to go to be able to feel included in America, while whites focus on how far we, as Americans, have come, and wonder why minorities don't just stop com-plaining and get over the past. There is truth in both of these realities. As a result, today, even more so than in the past, we have an opportunity to create a reality for America that we all can collectively envision—a reality in which people of color whine only when necessary and only when appropriate, and a reality in which whites acknowledge and not exude privilege. Ellis Cose, author, columnist, and contributing editor for *Newsweek,* states in his latest book, *The Envy of the World,* that although the obstacles for black Americans are not so daunting as in previous times, black Americans are still at a decided disadvantage. Cose describes the dif-ference as "stepping into the ring with both hands lashed behind your back and stepping in with one hand swinging free." If that description is indeed true for black Americans (and I believe it is), then in our world of increasing racial diversity, most white Americans go into the ring blind—and others without their glasses. Decades of discrimination have rendered some people of color into a group of whiners, many still exercising behaviors that were at one time adaptive but now are maladaptive. This same history has positioned white Americans repeatedly to fall comfortably on the soft pillow of privilege oblivious to the fact that the bed is no longer there. So, here is a formula for the interracial marriage of all Americans:

FOR PEOPLE OF COLOR:
Ten Easy Steps to Stop Whining

Know and learn your history. Separate facts from myths. There are great Web sites on the Internet today that make it easy to do this. Check out the history for yourself—read it yourself, or sit in a class and learn it for yourself.

Stay in the present. If there are lessons to be applied from history, they will be more apparent to you if you are focused in the present reality.

Do not pass ignorance on to your children. When you make generalizations to your children about white people and other racial groups different from your own, know that they are most likely listening to you and, more importantly accepting *your* experience as reality. Let them have their own experience and make their own reality.

Do not let the past determine the future for race relations in America. No one has a crystal ball, but everyone has free will.

Expect whites to have basic respect for human differences. You will more often find that it is true.

Do not put out negative energy about race. We used to tell one another, "Act your age and not your color." We should now proudly tell others to "Act your color."

Take the race card out of your deck. Do not play cards with people who aren't willing to play fair in the first place.

Challenge your assumptions. Accept someone else's opinions. Act on facts.

Listen for understanding, not rebuttal.

Own your sense of identity as an American—vote.

FOR WHITES:

How Not to Exude Privilege

Learn what racial privilege is, and examine expressions of it in your own life.

Engage in systems thinking. Understand your group-membership identity. Go around for one day thinking about yourself as a white person. Understand that just the fact that you need to heighten your awareness about whiteness is significant.

Do not get defensive in conversations about race. Own your reality of America, while at the same time acknowledging the reality of others.

Release the need to be right. Support dialogues that hold multiple realities.

Challenge your assumptions. Do not believe everything you were taught.

Stop whining yourself. You may not personally experience privilege afforded to you because of individual traits, but simply by being white, you have historically been afforded opportunities and treated more fairly than other racial groups.

Embrace whiteness fully. Be unapologetic about it. Being white is not synonymous with being an oppressor. Learn about your culture. Celebrate the contributions of whites.

Equal treatment does not mean identical treatment. Being in the majority does not mean ownership.

Do not rely on your good intentions to lessen a negative impact. Acknowledge that someone could have experienced something negatively, based on experience and history, regardless of your intention. Own that you might have contributed to that impact, despite your good intentions.

Become racially facile. Stay engaged during racial clashes. Do not be afraid to bring up a racial topic again and again until you are familiar with the script of multicultural living.

After decades of silence, in December 2003, Essie Mae Washington-Williams, a seventy-eight-year-old retired schoolteacher in Los Angeles, California, publicly revealed her relationship as the illegitimate, biracial daughter of Strom Thurmond. Strom Thurmond, the longest-serving senator in U.S. history, had run for president as a segregationist in 1948 and was opposed to the civil rights' programs. Carrie Butler, Essie Mae's mother, worked as a maid in the Thurmond family home in Edgefield, South Carolina. Carrie Butler was sixteen and Thurmond was twenty-two at the time of Essie Mae's birth.

Upon her public acknowledgement, some criticized Mrs. Washington-Williams for remaining silent for so long, believing her silence was motivated by money. Her critics further believed that an earlier claim to Senator Thurmond as her father could have been a powerful message and possibly changed the course of history. In my opinion, talking about what course history could have taken is an exercise of the imagination with no productive output for today. We are much better served by asking what message does Essie Mae Washington-Williams' disclosure have for race relations in 2004?

In her interview on *60 Minutes II*, correspondent Dan Rather asks Mrs. Washington-Williams "if in her mind and heart did she think Senator Thurmond was a racist?" Her response was, "I don't know that at heart he was. I think he did what he did to promote his career, but I never heard him using negative words or maybe statements about black people in general. He never did that. I don't believe he was a racist at heart. And when the times changed, he changed."

She kept her secret for sixty-two years and in her gentle manner chooses this time in history to set the record straight. What is clear is that in Essie Mae Washington-Williams' mind, Thurmond loved her and as a father, gave her what she needed. What we needed from Senator Thurmond as Americans may have been different. Nevertheless, her disclosure speaks to the ever-growing, complicated nature of race relations in America. I believe this is as powerful a message today as it would have been sixty-two years ago. Her disclosure is a wake-up call that we have to continue to unravel the dynamics of intentions and impact in our relationships and create societal structures that support individuals to speak their truth in the moment. Although we cannot change history, we do have the power today to create a history radically different from the legacy of the past.

As I explored for this book the roots of why we do not socialize across racial lines and reflected on my past beliefs about interracial marriages, I came to some profound personal insights. For many years, I wore the "I could never marry a white man" badge as a sign of racial pride. That badge really said more about my own unresolved racial identity—and the assumptions that I carried about white men—than it did about racial pride. I am glad to have dropped that kind of thinking. It has allowed me to be truly free and to walk with whomever I please, even without a destination. Some of my best friends are black, white, Asian, and Native American Indian. Despite the challenges, I would not have it any other way.

"Some of My Best Friends Are . . ." Journalogue

For Personal Reflection:

How are you exercising your inherent God-given right to fulfill your human potential by loving?

How are you whining as an American of color or exuding privilege as a white American?

By your example and encouragement, how do you support friendships and relationships that cross racial lines?

For Group Dialogue:

How do we, in our group membership identities, stop whining and/or exuding privilege?

What is necessary for your community to build an interracial bridge of understanding?

How is your faith community connected with other communities and establishing the interracial marriage of America?

For Spiritual Practice:

Spend a few moments in prayer and go about your day with an open heart, ready to be fully loved. Extend a gesture of welcome from your heart to someone across racial lines.

—ELEVEN—

Relief in Desert Places

Spirituality and Race Relations

THE MORE I WALK WITH Yvonne, the longer our walks get. She somehow feels she is conditioning me for some Olympic marathon or that walking is some kind of character-building experience. It reminds me of when I took Latin in ninth grade and was told I would never have to speak it (especially with black folks), but that learning Latin would be a good mental exercise. Our July 4th walk began early—at Yvonne's request—so that we would beat the heat anticipated for the day. Yet, she suggested, we could still start late enough so that we would have the benefit of sleeping in a bit on a non-working holiday. These kinds of requests and stipulations are always scary for me. It means that Yvonne does not have a time boundary and will be rested. This translates into endless walking. And so it was. We walked and walked and walked. The conversation was invigorating, yet after two hours, we were both parched. Yvonne decided that we should stop at the sighted Burger King for water. "Come on," she prodded, as I protested about not having any money with me, which was a weak attempt to get her to ask to use a phone to call for a return ride instead of asking for water. "Water will be free," she tells me. The cup of water generously given to us by the Burger King cashier was not only free but also provided the needed respite on the journey. Still, it was not until I arrived home that I felt that it was indeed Independence Day.

In today's world, we need relief from its existence to feel truly free. My friend Jacquie tells me that she can no longer watch the news before she goes to bed. The images and words of violence dance through her head, making her sleep fretful at best. I have a similar response to images and words presented in the media and, because of what I do for a living, I am especially sensitive to issues of diversity, particularly racial issues. Somehow, I have not mastered the psychological distance required as a therapist that allows me to work with patients and not let their problems become my problems when it comes to race relations. Every newspaper article that I read about race demands from me an internal, and sometimes external, response. With every television or radio show about race, I become a participant observer. Like Pavlov's dog, I am conditioned to react. My reactions often lead to depressed and hopeless feelings. Then I pray; then, I spend time with my friends.

I am truly blessed to have many good friends and a critical component of that blessing is that they cross racial lines. I could not have sustained twenty years of professional practice of diversity without these people in my life. The media constantly and consistently reminds me that the racial divide is deeply apparent in how life in the United States is lived and expressed. My work in corporate America validates what I hear on the television news and read in the newspapers. My friends remind me of a different reality and are my relief in the desert of America's divided race relations.

The vocalist, Kem, on his CD *Kemistry,* composes and sings "This Place," a song written about his faith community, The Church of Today. In praising its diversity, he sings of a universal need for "this place." "The place" of racial inclusion has its roots in spirituality. Just as racism is fundamentally a spiritual problem, racial inclusion can only result from that which transcends our earthly nature. In the Christian tradition, we are reminded by Paul, the apostle, that we are citizens of heaven. This citizenship is not one governed by human leaders, fueled by politics, and characterized by marginalization of the have-nots and less-thans. We are challenged to become part of this citizenship based on love of God. The more we love, the more we enjoy the benefits of heavenly citizenship.

Father Thomas Judge, founder of the religious order of Missionary Servants of the Most Holy Trinity, writes that the church is essentially the meeting place of the souls God created. No matter what class, what generation, what color, each one of us is called to be a saint in God's church. We magnify God by magnifying his saints. In other words, church is a meeting place of friends or saints.

I know that it may be hard to think of some of our friends as "saints," but in the context of being citizens of heaven, that is indeed what we are. Spending time with friends, with saints, connects us to God. Greg

Kandra, a story producer for the CBS news program, *60 Minutes II* states it eloquently in an article published in *America:*

> For friendship is, at its best, a prayer. It is sacred. It is an epistle, delivered from one person to another. In its best moments, friendship is a canticle that celebrates, a parable that teaches. In the case of proximity of a friend, you find a cathedral where promises are kept, and a chapel where tears are shed. Friendship is a responsorial psalm: one heart speaks, another responds, and in the silences in between we hear something of God.

God speaks to us through our friendships, and those that cross racial lines allow us to experience the citizenship of heaven. Unfortunately, for too long in the United States, churches—the meeting places of the saints—have been racially exclusive in terms of their membership, ministry, and mission. Most of us who are churchgoers attend churches that are not diverse and race is rarely, if ever, mentioned as a topic of interest or pursuit. In Shreveport, Louisiana, Bishop Fred Caldwell, after unsuccessfully urging his white friends to join, decided to pay whites to attend the five thousand predominately black membership of Greenwood Acres Full Gospel Baptist Church in order to reach his dream of "a rainbow in God's church." Along with some media attention for his offer, some whites agreed to come for free.

There are some faith traditions where the heavenly vision of racial unity does not come with an offer of payment. One such faith community in the Christian tradition is the United Church of Christ. I was first introduced to the United Church of Christ (UCC) through Edith Guffey. At that time, she was the community's National Secretary and noted in *Ebony* magazine as one of the one hundred most influential blacks in the church. Edith had requested that I facilitate a dialogue on racism with their administrative council. In preparing for this intervention, I became enraptured with tenets of this religion. The United Church of Christ was founded in 1957 as the union of several different Christian traditions: Congregational, Christian, Evangelical, and Reformed. Now one of the most diverse Christian churches in the United States, the United Church of Christ is known for many diversity "firsts." Among these "firsts" are some noted ones on race: an early stand against slavery; first published

African American poet; first ordained African American pastor; and the church recognized for paying the one million dollar bail for Benjamin Chavis, the civil rights activist whose conviction was successfully overturned.

Since 1957, the United Church of Christ has struggled to define, shape, understand, and direct itself to the end "that they all may be one." They have pronounced themselves to be a multiracial and multicultural church. This "living pronouncement" is considered vital to their wholeness and existence as a community of faith. By embodying diversity as gifts to the human family, UCC members rejoice in the variety of God's graces. And rejoice they do.

Since my first intervention with UCC members, I have had other opportunities to work with this faith community in their efforts to become a multiracial, multicultural church. My experiences have introduced me to others, like Edith, now Associate General Minister, and Bernice Powell Jackson, Executive Minister of Justice and Witness Ministries, who are faith-filled and "radically committed" to ending racism and the barriers that divide people because of race. It is an example of relief in a desert place to know that there is a faith tradition where Jesus' prayer "that they all may be one" is front and center to its mission.

Another faith tradition in which racial unity is not only a vision but also a reality is the Baha'i faith. A recent news magazine reported a growing trend of whites in attendance at historically black colleges and universities (HBCUs). In the article, a young white male is asked what motivates him to attend an HBCU. He reports that there was no dilemma in his choice and he experienced no discomfort in his attendance in an environment where he was the racial minority. At this point in my reading, I guessed that it must be his faith that allowed him to be so counterculture in his actions. Knowing Melodie and Richard Yates, my introducers to the Baha'i faith, I thought to myself, "He must be a Baha'i." Sure enough, in completing the article, the interviewer credits the young man's Baha'i faith as the catalyst for his choice.

The Baha'i religion is an independent, monotheistic, world religion. As the youngest of the world's independent religions, it is the second most widespread. Baha'is follow the teachings of Bahaullah who lived from 1817 to 1892, and its members embody "the principle of equal opportunity, rights and privileges for both sexes, advocates compulsory education, abolishes extremes of poverty and wealth, recommends the adoption of an auxiliary international language, and provides the necessary agencies for the establishment and safeguarding of a permanent and universal peace." Oneness of humanity is a central principle of the faith, thus where there are Baha'is, there is diversity.

Most Baha'is, like Melodie and Richard Yates, came to the Baha'i faith as a way to worship God that followed the manner in which they were already living their life. Melodie and Richard, an interracial couple married for over twenty-five years, have been Baha'is most of their married life. "When we had children," Richard tells me, "we felt like we had to have a spiritual group where our kids would feel whole." In my research for this book, I wanted to hear more about the Baha'i faith, especially its expression of racial unity, and I asked Melodie to gather some Baha'is for me to interview.

This turned out to be a very easy task for Melodie to accomplish, for Baha'is seem to naturally gather for fellowship in the timing of a heart-beat. Melodie was only limited by the size of their family room in the number of people to invite. An invitation meant an automatic "yes" response. So, I gathered one evening with twelve members of the Baha'i faith in Melodie and Richard's family room for more learning about the Baha'i faith's quest for racial unity in the context of spirituality and how friendships nourished this belief.

Not surprisingly, it was by socializing in diverse groups that most of these persons came to know of the Baha'i faith or, if Baha'i from birth, their faith had made them automatically a part of a diverse environment. Susanne, a forty-seven-year-old white woman, states, "I grew up in Canada in an all-white environment. When my parents became Baha'i, all of a sudden there were people in our home from all races. I can't imagine going back to anything different. It would be like taking a rainbow and taking all the colors out of it." Barbara, another participant, affirms that when the Baha'is come together, it is like "a big family reunion and just not knowing all the family yet."

Emma recalls the time when she attempted to move away from her family tradition of racial diversity by becoming a black nationalist in the 1960s.

> I grew up in a Baha'i family. There were Negroes, Jews, and whites. The house that had everybody [coming] in and out was my home. Anywhere [where] my mom has been in this country, we spent time at the Baha'i place of worship. After I became an adult and tried to become a black

nationalist, I found out they didn't want me. So, I moved to Atlanta. I got off the bus and my reaction was WHOA! It was wall-to-wall black people. I'd never seen that before. I moved on and met two white folks. The neighborhood they took me to was all black folks. So, twelve hours later I came back here to Cleveland, because I had never been in a segregated neighborhood before [this time]. I had always lived in integrated neighborhoods and gone to integrated schools.

At sixty-five years of age, Emma can still not imagine a one-race environment. Her faith tells her she does not have to try.

Jan, a forty-two-year-old white woman, tells me that the experience of richness of culture that she has found in the Baha'i faith makes her feel like she is in a cultural vacuum if she is in a monoracial setting. Married to Farid, an Iranian who grew up in the Baha'i faith, she now lives in a community in which they have to make an effort to have diverse interactions. However, as a result of their marriage and being Baha'is, Jan and Farid's children have grown up "knowing how to switch cultures."

After almost an hour of "sugar and spice and everything nice" responses, I challenged their pronouncements of what appeared to be an easy accomplishment of racial harmony. They quickly retorted with testimonies to the difficulty of racial harmony even when motivated by faith. Nevin, an energetic twenty-nine-year-old whose mother, Mary Lou, tells me that she has to remind him that he is white, responds that their responses may sound flowery but that it is easy to socialize with people who believe the way you do. He believes that we teach ignorance to our kids by passing on stereotypes and myths. As a teacher, he works to eradicate these messages.

Pat, a fifty-two-year-old black woman, places the challenge of racial unity in the context of prayer. "Being a Baha'i allows me to pray a lot in a situation. Sometimes hearing we are not one race is a test. I pray that at one point we will be, but I also look at the reality of the situation." Looking at Pat as she sat between her seventy-eight-year-old mother, Bernice, and her eighty-two-year-old father, Pleasant, I knew that her faith had to be solid. Her parents shared stories of their early years as Baha'is when police were called because there were blacks socializing in the homes of whites for Baha'i gatherings. I am convinced that her parents' many years of prayer and faith conviction are the source of Pat's continued prayerful response to racial strife and tension.

The spiritual context in which Baha'is live and work is the source of their hope for racial unity. Melodie tells me that it is not that they are "not of the world. We bring our biases and prejudices like everyone else, and because of our faith, we keep plowing away at ridding ourselves of them. We pray."

In June 2003, I had the distinct honor of attending the General Chapter of the Missionary Servants of the Most Holy Trinity as a lay delegate. General Chapters are meetings of religious orders that set the direction for the community for the next five years. The lay delegates were full participants in all the activities of the chapter, although not voting members. On the day of the community's election of new council members, all the delegates gathered at the chapel of Father Thomas Judge in Holy Trinity Alabama. The chapel was once the two-room home of Father Judge when he came to Alabama to serve the poor and the abandoned in 1909. The homily for the liturgy was given by Brother Richard who told the story of a town of people with no shoes that was also home to one of the largest shoe factories in the world. When the townspeople were repeatedly confronted about getting shoes to protect their feet, their standard response was, "Yes, why don't we?" And they would continue to go about their lives shoeless. Brother Richard posed the same question to us as people of faith in a world of disbelief. Why don't we live our lives in a way that conforms to our faith?

June, a forty-seven-year-old black woman, tells me that when her second daughter went to school in Boston she wore a Baha'i T-shirt that said, "One World, One People." Someone approached her and said, "That's really deep." "No," June laughs, "that's really simple."

It is simple if we pray. It is simple if we embrace race relations from a spiritual framework. It is simple if we have friends—saints of all races who are also praying for one world, one people.

"Relief in Desert Places" Journalogue

For Personal Reflection:

Reflect on your friends as saints. In what way are they allowing you to realize racial unity?

Think of a recent news event that involved race. Place it in a spiritual context. What difference does this make to your thoughts about the issue and your response?

For Group Dialogue:

Tell how God, through your cross-racial friendships, manifests hope.

If racism is a spiritual problem, how are you and others you know, working through your faith to eradicate it?

What do faith communities, yours in particular, need to know and do to establish racial harmony? How do you see your friendships and socializing across racial lines supporting this?

For Spiritual Practice:

Living a spiritual life calls us to reflect the freedom of God's unconditional love. Forgive someone for their racial biases by befriending them.

—TWELVE—

Overcoming Laziness

Challenges and Benefits of Socializing across Racial Lines

YVONNE ALWAYS GIVES ME A CHOICE when we are walking. After we have gotten started and already ventured into areas that are unrecognizable to me, the choices come. The choices are about what path we will take. "We can go down this street," she will instruct me, "but there is a steep hill. Or we can go this way, but it will take us about ten minutes longer to get back." Some choice. Either way I will be physically strained. This is when I usually start complaining. I tell her that I need to carry my cell phone with me so that when she gets me too far out, I can call somebody to pick me up. I threatened to flag down the car of the first person I might remotely recognize and catch a ride back. I quiz her about how far it is to a certain friend's house, so that I can figure out whether to stop there instead of walking all the way back. Yvonne just laughs and keeps me moving. Once I stop complaining and get moving, I become involved in our conversation and begin to forget about the distance. The more we walk, the less I complain. When we return home, I feel great. I feel as if I have won an Olympic gold medal for a marathon.

Maintaining friendships that cross racial lines present a constant challenge. We can't be lazy about it. The probability of bumping up against the race wall increases with every contact made with someone who is racially different from us. Certainly, most people today are not racist—at least in the classical sense of the term "racism." Overt, intentional racism (cross burnings, lynchings, denial of memberships based on race) does still exist today. In June 2003, two white men in Huntsville, Alabama, were sentenced to 8 and 11 years in prison for burning a cross in a yard of a white woman whose black friends visited her home. Thank God, we, as a people, are collectively horrified when this kind of situation happens.

However, covert, unintentional racism, such as racial profiling, being ignored for service because of race, having a negative personality trait ascribed to an entire race, and exclusionary mentoring practices, abounds. Racist covert (attitudinal, internal) and unintentional (not in the person's conscious awareness and not the professed outcome desired) behaviors are harder for the perpetrators to own and are psychologically confusing for their recipients. In social situations when one's defenses are down—and usually one's thinking capacity, as well—slip ups can happen. No one likes or wants this kind of stress in a social situation. Avoiding one another socially is one way of solving the dilemma. In my opinion, it is not the best way, and certainly, it is not the most rewarding way.

My sister, Nancy, has worked in retail management most of her professional life. At one time, she worked for a company in which she was the only black employee in her local office. There was another woman named Nancy in that office. The receptionist often had to ask clients who came to the office to see "Nancy"—not providing the last name, "Which one?" My sister told me that more times than she could count, the person (always white) would lean over the desk and whisper, "The black one." This became such a joke in the office that the Nancys would then be called "black Nancy" and "white Nancy," with race being part of their name identification. If a person would whisper, "the black one," the receptionist would yell out, "black Nancy," only to the great chagrin of the client.

I imagine that in whispering the word *black,* the client thought he or she was being color-blind and therefore more racially sensitive. However, whispering "black," as if the term was a derogatory word, implies that there is something wrong with being black. When a person tries to be "color-blind," it generally leads to the exact opposite effect. The people in my sister's office were comfortable enough with each other that race was no more than an identifier. In fact, "white Nancy" and "black Nancy" remain friends today, despite the fact that they no longer work together and my sister now lives in a different state. The "color-blind" approach is one of the many ways we have handled our racial differences, and it has been considered by many to be forward thinking because it de-emphasizes racial differences and emphasizes racial similarities. In theory, it appears to be affirming diversity, but in practice, it demonstrates a hierarchical and patronizing approach. In other words, in order for me as a white American to deal with you as a person of color, I have to pretend that I do not see color but only see the ways in which we are the same. In reality, I see that you are a person of color but I relate to you as if you were just like me.

Here are some other approaches we have tried. The race-deficient approach was popular in the 1960s through the 1970s and is still alive in the hearts and minds of many social service workers and churchgoing people. Any race that is not white American is considered to be lacking in cultural strengths, and therefore the best approach to dealing with those who are racially different is to provide them with education and opportunities for cultural development. This approach is consistent with an assimilation model and the melting-pot theory. Minorities simply needed to "melt" their differences and become like majority culture.

Unfortunately, this approach remains active today. Here is a present-day example. Many times in consulting, I have had to work with people to help them understand the differences in time orientation that races carry with them to the work setting and other group gatherings. "Why are they [blacks, Hispanics] always late?" a white man asked. "Well," I responded, "On the individual level, I am sure there are a whole host of reasons why someone might be considered late, but we do know something about cultural patterns of time orientation from the research. It is likely that many African Americans, Asian Americans, and Latino Americans are circular-time people. That means that time is perceived as a movement that is a repeated cycle. Each moment is important, so you are fully present to the experience in that moment. An activity takes as much time as needed for its completion before you move on to the next activity. Since time is circular, if you miss something, it will come around again. It's like the seasons and the process of farming—you plant, you cultivate, and you harvest—then you do it all again. Most white Americans think of time as fixed points—past, present, and future. If you miss the moment, it will never come back. It is in the past. From this perspective, it is important to make every minute count and to get the most out of the time you have. So when you schedule a meeting or expect some people of color to arrive at a specific time—they may simply translate this to be the time for gathering or they may consider it an approximate starting time. The business that needs to take place can only happen when those who need to be there are all fully present." I could see that the members of this group—all white—were carefully considering what was being said. I encouraged them to consider time to be a negotiable concept. Do not assume that everyone is on the same page just because a time has been announced. When you are working with diverse populations and in global settings, be careful not to label someone as lazy or irresponsible because they value work outcomes more than being bound by "clock time." If the work product or outcome is excellent and meets agreed-upon needs, what does clock time matter?

After our discussion, I thought the participants had "gotten it" until I heard later that when I left, they were quick to joke, "Hell, I don't believe that stuff on time orientation. THEY have been in this country long enough,—don't you think THEY should have adapted by now."

My questions are: Whose country is it? Who is doing all the adapting? It does not presume or even mean that in predominately black or Hispanic settings that there will not be disagreements and even heated debates (as in my parish community) of the starting time for worship services and meetings. My point is, to presume that one orientation or way of knowing is *the* only one and *the* best approach is naïve and inappropriate in a multicultural world.

Another approach to managing race differences is the race-denial approach. This approach puts emphasis on race sameness but instead of being blind to color, we deny that color even exists. "We are all human beings." "We are all Americans." "We all put our pants on the same way." "We all have red blood inside." The denial of our racial heritage and the historical impact and variance in the experience of American dreams and ideals are forever strong in this approach. It is impossible to have interracial friendships from this perspective because somebody (and we can all guess who that somebody might be) has to give up the uniqueness of who they are as a racial being. Many people of color feel it is hard to maintain their friendships with whites because they are always working to make white people feel comfortable. Unless they choose activities, locations, and events in which whites are in the majority, whites are simply uncomfortable.

I am most fond of the racial-tourist approach because it usually involves food. This approach emphasizes the strengths of each racial group by celebrating differences through sharing our cultures. We "visit" one another's cultures as welcomed guests. Our gospel choir goes and sings at your suburban white church. Everyone at work brings in a dish to share from his or her culture, and we get together at lunchtime. Don't get me wrong: This is a good start but it is simplistic in orientation. It often does not lead people to deal with the differences in racial expression of cultural values and norms that are generally the source of racial clashes and miscommunication. If I visit your church for a multicultural feast and I ask why you moved to a new neighborhood when two black families moved onto your street, you may start to feel as if you need some Pepto-Bismol.

We use these approaches because we are lazy, because they are simple approaches, and because we don't know a better approach. We rarely learn diversity competencies in any formal setting, such as school or professional training classes, so we have to wing it. And we make mistakes when we wing it. Making mistakes doesn't feel good, so we stay away from situations in which we are known to make mistakes. We stay away from people who do not look like us.

Yet we know that it is getting harder and harder to avoid one another. Today, you have to be pretty creative if you are white and want to stay away from people of color. Similarly, you have to work hard to keep away from whites if you are a person of color. Trust me, it would take more energy to keep dodging than it would to learn some simple diversity skills. What is simple, I acknowledge, is not always the easiest to do. It requires time, sensitivity, non-defensiveness, and making choices that may perhaps disappoint others when a "diversity choice" is selected over a more familiar and expected choice. These simple choices, however, yield huge results.

Here are some simple choices:

Learn the value of a variety of opinions and thoughts. See "the other side of the dollar bill."

Recognize the challenges and learning opportunities that new perspectives bring. Where there is discomfort there is learning, if we stay with the discomfort long enough.

Base your expectations of others on individual qualities and traits rather than racial group identity.

Seek out ways to personally and professionally develop diversity competencies. Take a class, watch a video, read a book on racial issues.

Encourage and accept openness in others. Do not assume.

When you make a mistake that involves race—get over it! Become emotionally resilient. Learn from it and move on.

Spend time with a variety of people—don't avoid situations or events in which you might be the "only one" or one of a few.

Make other people feel valued. It will increase your own sense of worth.

Have a clear sense of yourself as a racial being. Understand how race has affected your life and influenced your thinking and behavior. Stop being an expert on what the other race is thinking.

Talk with and socialize with your friends of different races. Don't be afraid to ask the stupid questions. Don't be afraid to give the honest responses.

I began this book by building a rationale for why I believe it is important to have friends and to socialize across racial lines. I stated that it was not necessary but clearly beneficial to do so. It is the "not necessary" part that presents the challenge, and if we do not embrace this, we will close ourselves off from any possibility of discovering the benefits of a different way of being. Not only do we thwart our personal growth, but our spiritual identity also diminishes without this dimension in our lives.

Receiving those benefits is worth any challenge that needs to be faced. A few years ago, the religious community to which I once belonged invited all of its former nuns back for a day of renewal and healing. I reluctantly decided to go after some prodding from my friend, Father Mike. I did not hold any ill feeling at all toward any of the sisters as individuals, but the community was a symbol of a great deal of pain for me concerning issues of racial inclusion and acceptance (as a vast majority of the religious community in the 1970s would have also been). I did not want all that pain stirred up again. Still, a day of renewal and healing sounded like a good place to start to get rid of it. Once I got there, I enjoyed seeing the remodeled building and appreciated the warm, loving welcome from members of my former community. A profoundly healing experience for me was my visit with the elderly and sick sisters in the infirmary. As Sister Margaret Hess escorted me through the facility, I encountered many familiar faces, older now. Many, of course, remembered me—or at least remembered my racial identity. I felt a special connection to these sisters who were in the last phases of their life here on earth because my dad had suffered a long illness and had died just a few months earlier. I was reminded that in the end, no matter what color we are, we must all experience the same journey home. These sisters were living in a way that made them ready to die. Their promises of prayer for me buoyed my spirits and sent me back home with renewed hope.

One of the greatest gifts we can give one another as human beings is the gift of friendship. The spiritual writer Henri Nouwen states that friendships create a bond beyond common goals, common interests, or common histories. He believes that friendship is a bond that is stronger than a sexual union can create and deeper than a shared fate can solidify. Pretty powerful.

I reimagine the world of my elementary school years: Carlos Roland, Judy Schwelgien, Maria Mabini, Gayle Starling, Michael Easler, Deborah Harris, and Cheryl Maxwell were all in the same classroom. White, black, Asian, Latino—all there. I dream of a world that would have treated us all the same, skin color notwithstanding, and in my vision, we became adults who do not hold barriers based on race that would prevent us from being friends again.

I am fortunate to have retained many of my childhood friends into adulthood. Of my elementary school days, I remain friends with Gayle, Debbie, and Cheryl (who now uses her first name of Zoë). Of my high school friends Joan, Rita, and Michelle, I see Joan and Rita frequently, and Michelle less often, since she lives across town and is raising four children. Yet, we all managed to get together to celebrate Joan's and Rita's fiftieth birthday.

I have a great deal of contact with Zoë (who is black) and Joan (who is white). Zoë and I are in the same women's volunteer group, we are involved with our moms in another club, and we talk a lot about politics, theology, and social concerns. Joan and I have served on the same advisory committees, we have shared the same stresses of providing support to our aging parents, and we talk a lot about politics, theology, and social concerns. The dynamics of the two relationships don't seem very different. Race doesn't change the interests or personalities. The appearances and the personality styles of my friends may be different, but the substance of the friendships is the same.

My family and I received a lot of support from friends of many colors when my dad became terminally ill. His wake was a memorial not just to my dad's good spirit but also to the spirit of humankind. I had expected to see those of my friends who were actively involved in my everyday life, but I was also gifted by the presence of many who had shared different phases of life's journey with me. There was the presence of the St. Thomas Aquinas community of more than thirty years ago—my third and eighth grade teachers, Sisters Lucy and Ruth, and Mrs. Reinhard, The Starlings, and Mike Haggerty. There was the presence of the many, many Sisters of Notre Dame, my former religious community. There was the presence of former and present students. There was the presence of my black friends, white friends, Asian friends, Latino friends, and Native American Indian friends. About a week later, I ran into Sue Cicero (who is white) at the mall. There are many ties between us. Sue had been in high school with my sister Nancy. I had taught her sister Eileen in my early teaching days, and Eileen and I remain friends. Sue and I taught together on the same faculty when she began teaching. I know her parents; I had shopped in her mom's religious bookstore. Nowadays, her daughter, Colleen, is the best friend of my niece, Mercedes. Sue had brought Colleen and another friend of Mercedes' to my dad's wake. (These teens had taken the time to make a collage of quotes to comfort Mercedes on the loss of her beloved grandfather.) In addition, Sue and Colleen were also present at my dad's funeral Mass. I told Sue how grateful I was for the support she had shown and how impressed I was at the message she is teaching Colleen. She told me how important she thought it was to teach teens what to do to comfort one another at these times. "It [the funeral] was just as I imagined. I told Colleen to expect to see a whole lot of different people there. That's what you get with the Plummers."

I have learned a lot from my friends of color. They help me to see the world in a very real way. They challenge the internalized racism that creeps in when I become enmeshed in the predictable media presentations of race or when I am blinded by the one-sided pictures of the world that my socioeconomic level allows me to see. They support my psyche and help me to know that I am not alone in how I have experienced the world. They help me not to take life so seriously—and to laugh and laugh and laugh. They provide constant reminders that we have overcome—that overcoming is not about doing better than or competing with white folks (they are not even in the picture); overcoming is about remaining true to who you are in all your glory. They have been proud of me, and they have taught me how to have pride in myself. They keep me faithful and faith-filled. They bring God's presence to me, again and again.

I have learned a lot from my white friends. They remind me of the universal nature of joy and sorrow. They help me to see the bigger picture.

They challenge my intellectual faculties and stimulate my curiosity. They have taught me the art of appreciation. They have uncovered my sense of personal power. They have taught me how to use power in a way that is mutually beneficial. They have shown me how to be supportive by showing me support—even when they "don't get it." They have given me the experience of pure goodness, again and again. They have believed in me and taught me how to believe in myself. They have blessed me and shown me God's blessing.

Everyone wins when we race through this life with friends of many races. Crossing racial lines in friendships takes time to build understanding. It requires patience to learn how to trust; it is often exhausting when we try to communicate effectively; and it is often painful when there are racial clashes. Yet, all the time, energy, and personal expense spent in running through life with cross-racial friendships are so worthwhile. We experience the joys of true friendship when we successfully cross the racial finish line.

Paul, in his writings to the church at Philippi, speaks of his longing to know Christ and the power of the resurrection. Paul tells his friends that he is "still running, trying to capture the prize for which Christ captured him." This prize, Paul tells us, can only be won by forgetting the past and straining ahead for what is still to come. "Racing for the finish, for the prize to which God calls us." When we are running in this kind of race, our friends of many races and nations are truly our joy and our crown.

"Overcoming Laziness" Journalogue

For Personal Reflection:

What challenges are present to you in cross-racial friendships? What means do you use to overcome them?

Which of the simple choices have you made recently? What was the outcome?

What simple choices are you committed to trying?

For Group Dialogue:

What approach to diversity has your faith community engaged in?

What approach do you wish to embrace? What will it take to implement it?

For Spiritual Practice:

Pray the "Palms Up/Palms Down" exercise. Place your palms up and symbolically place in your hands all that challenges you about racial diversity and that which maintains your laziness about socializing across racial lines. Then place your palms down as a symbol of releasing all of these concerns. Spend a few moments in prayer for racial unity.

RELATED TITLES FROM
The Pilgrim Press

DISMANTLING PRIVILEGE

An Ethics of Accountability

Mary Elizabeth Hobgood

This book explores the unearned advantages held by those who are privileged by class, race, and gender. It also uncovers the steady erosion of these privileges, demonstrates how the privileged are damaged by present arrangements even as they benefit from them, and shows that the best solution is a politics of solidarity.

ISBN 0-8298-1374-8
Paper, 192 pages
$20.00

ENDING RACISM IN
THE CHURCH

Susan E. Davies and Sister Paul Teresa Hennessee, S.A., eds.

This resource is an invaluable aid to church members of all backgrounds. It raises awareness of how racism influences behavior and spawns hatred. Four case studies describe church or community agencies that strive to end racism, and a diverse group of scholars and activists identify the subtle ways in which racism undermines the gospel's spirit.

ISBN 0-8298-1238-5
Paper, 160 pages
$13.00

SAY IT LOUD

Middle-Class Blacks talk about Racism and What to Do about It

Annie S. Barnes

The author has solicited the stories of 150 black college students from middle-class backgrounds, who tell of their frequent encounters with racism —at school, at work, in their neighborhoods, at restaurants and shopping malls. Through their disquieting testimony, the daily indignities that black Americans still suffer are brought to light.

ISBN 0-8298-1336-5
Paper, 192 pages
$17.00

To order these or any other books from **The Pilgrim Press**, *call or write to:*

The Pilgrim Press
700 Prospect Avenue E
Cleveland, OH 44115-1100

Phone orders: 800.537.3394
(M-F, 8:30am-4:30pm ET)
Fax orders: 216.736.2206

Please include shipping charges of $5.00 for the first book and 75¢ for each additional book.

Or order from our Web site at www.thepilgrimpress.com.

Prices subject to change without